Holt Geometry

Know-It Notebook™

HOLT, RINEHART AND WINSTON

A Harcourt Education Company

Orlando • **Austin** • New York • San Diego • London

ISBN 978-0-03-078092-9
ISBN 0-03-078092-6

4 5 6 7 8 9   862   09 08

Contents

Geometry

USING THE *KNOW-IT NOTEBOOK*™

This *Know-It Notebook* will help you take notes, organize your thinking, and study for quizzes and tests. There are *Know-It Notes*™ pages for every lesson in your textbook. These notes will help you identify important mathematical information that you will need later.

Know-It Notes

Vocabulary

One good note-taking practice is to keep a list of the new vocabulary.

- Use the page references or the glossary in your textbook to find each definition and a clarifying example.
- Write each definition and example on the lines provided.

Lesson Objectives

Another good note-taking practice is to know the objective the content covers.

Key Concepts

Key concepts from each lesson are included. They are indicated in your book with the KIN logo.

- Write each answer in the space provided.
- Check your answers with your book.
- Ask your teacher to help you with any concept that you don't understand.

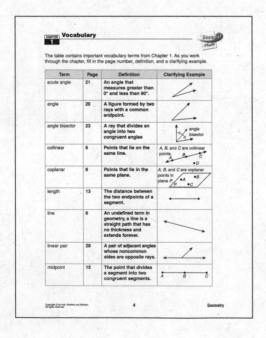

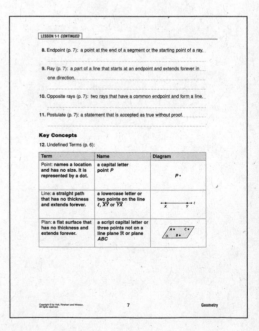

Geometry

Chapter Review

Complete Chapter Review problems that follow each chapter. This is a good review before you take the chapter test.

- Write each answer in the space provided.
- Check your answers with your teacher or another student.
- Ask your teacher to help you understand any problem that you answered incorrectly.

Postulates and Theorems

A list of the postulates and theorems are included for each chapter as they are introduced.

Big Ideas

The Big Ideas have you summarize the important chapter concepts in your own words. You must think about and understand ideas to put them in your words. This will also help you remember them.

- Write each answer in the space provided.
- Check your answers with your teacher or another student.
- Ask your teacher to help you understand any question that you answered incorrectly.

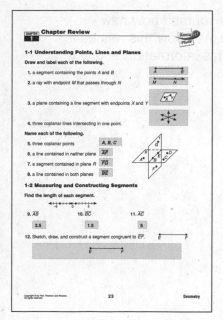

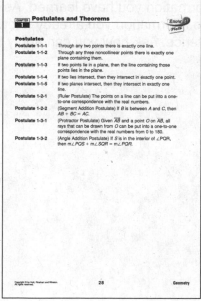

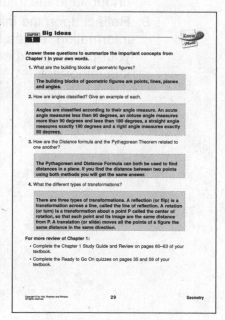

Geometry

NOTE TAKING STRATEGIES

Taking good notes is very important in many of your classes and will be even more important when you take college classes. This notebook was designed to help you get started. Here are some other steps that can help you take good notes.

Getting Ready

1. Use a loose-leaf notebook. You can add pages to this where and when you want to. It will help keep you organized.

During the Lecture

2. If you are taking notes during a lecture, write the big ideas. Use abbreviations to save time. Do not worry about spelling or writing every word. Use headings to show changes in the topics discussed. Use numbering or bullets to organize supporting ideas under each topic heading. Leave space before each new heading so that you can fill in more information later.

After the Lecture

3. As soon as possible after the lecture, read through your notes and add any information that will help you understand so that when you review later, they make sense. You should also summarize the information into key words or key phrases. This will help your comprehension and will help you process the information. These key words and key phrases will be your memory cues when you are reviewing for taking a test. At this time you may also want to write questions to help clarify the meaning of the ideas and facts.

4. Read your notes out loud. As you do this, state the ideas in your own words and do as much as you can by memory. This will help you remember and will also help with your thinking process. This activity will help you understand the information.

5. Reflect upon the information you have learned. Ask yourself how new information relates to information you already know. Ask how this relates to your personal experience. Ask how you can apply this information and why it is important.

Geometry

Before the Test

6. Review your notes. Don't wait until the night before the test to review. Do frequent reviews. Don't just read through your notes. Put the information in your notes into your own words. If you do this you will be able to connect the new material with material you already know and you will be better prepared for tests. You will have less test anxiety and better recall.

7. Summarize your notes. This should be in your own words and should only include the main points you need to remember. This will help you internalize the information.

Geometry

The table contains important vocabulary terms from Chapter 1. As you work through the chapter, fill in the page number, definition, and a clarifying example.

Term	Page	Definition	Clarifying Example
acute angle			
angle			
angle bisector			
collinear			
coplanar			
length			
line			
linear pair			
midpoint			

Geometry

Term	Page	Definition	Clarifying Example
obtuse angle			
plane			
point			
postulate			
ray			
right angle			
segment bisector			
straight angle			
vertical angles			

Geometry

Understanding Points, Lines, and Planes

Lesson Objectives (p. 6):

_____

_____

_____

Vocabulary

1. Undefined term (p. 6): _____

_____

_____

2. Point (p. 6): _____

_____

3. Line (p. 6): _____

_____

4. Plane (p. 6): _____

_____

5. Collinear (p. 6): _____

_____

6. Coplanar (p. 6): _____

_____

7. Segment (p. 7): _____

_____

_____

Geometry

8. Endpoint (p. 7): _____

_____

9. Ray (p. 7): _____

_____

_____

10. Opposite rays (p. 7): _____

_____

11. Postulate (p. 7): _____

_____

Key Concepts

12. Undefined Terms (p. 6):

Term	Name	Diagram
Point:		
Line:		
Plane:		

Geometry

13. Segments and Rays (p. 7):

Definition	Name	Diagram
Segment:		
Endpoint:		
Ray:		
Opposite rays:		

14. Postulates—Points, Lines and Planes (p. 7):

1-1-1

1-1-2

1-1-3

15. Postulates—Intersection of Lines and Planes (p. 8):

1-1-4
1-1-5

16. Get Organized In each box name, describe, and illustrate one of the undefined terms. (p. 8).

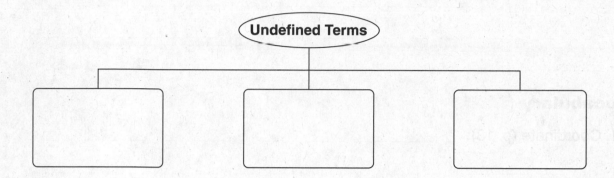

Measuring and Constructing Segments

Lesson Objectives (p. 13):

_____

_____

_____

Vocabulary

1. Coordinate (p. 13): _____

_____

2. Distance (p. 13): _____

_____

_____

3. Length (p. 13): _____

_____

4. Congruent segments (p. 13): _____

_____

5. Construction (p. 14): _____

_____

6. Between (p. 14): _____

_____

_____

7. Midpoint (p. 15): _____

_____

_____

Geometry

8. Bisect (p. 15): _____

_____

9. Segment bisector (p. 16): _____

_____

_____

Key Concepts

10. Postulate—Ruler Postulate (p. 13):

1-2-1

11. Postulate—Segment Addition Postulate (p. 14):

1-2-2

12. Get Organized Make a sketch and write an equation to describe each relationship. (p. 16).

	B is between *A* and *C*	*B* is the midpoint of $\overline{AC}$
Sketch		
Equation		

Geometry

Measuring and Constructing Angles

Lesson Objectives (p. 20):

_____

_____

Vocabulary

1. Angle (p. 20): _____

_____

2. Vertex (p. 20): _____

_____

3. Interior of an angle (p. 20): _____

_____

4. Exterior of an angle (p. 20): _____

_____

5. Measure (p. 20): _____

_____

6. Degree (p. 20): _____

_____

7. Acute angle (p. 21): _____

_____

8. Right angle (p. 21): _____

_____

9. Obtuse angle (p. 21): _____

_____

10. Straight angle (p. 21): _____

_____

Geometry

11. Congruent angles (p. 22): _____

_____

12. Angle bisector (p. 23): _____

_____

Key Concepts

13. Postulate—Protractor Postulate (p. 20):

1-3-1

14. Types of Angles (p. 21):

Geometry

15. Postulate—Angle Addition Postulate (p. 22):

1-3-2

16. Get Organized In the cells sketch, measure, and name an example of each angle type. (p. 24).

	DIAGRAM	MEASURE	NAME
Acute Angle			
Right Angle			
Obtuse Angle			
Straight Angle			

Geometry

Pairs of Angles

Lesson Objectives (p. 28):

_____

_____

Vocabulary

1. Adjacent angles (p. 28): _____

_____

2. Linear pair (p. 28): _____

_____

3. Complementary angles (p. 29): _____

_____

4. Supplementary angles (p. 29): _____

_____

5. Vertical angles (p. 30): _____

_____

Key Concepts

6. Pairs of Angles (p. 28):

Geometry

7. Complementary and Supplementary Angles (p. 29):

8. Get Organized In each box, draw a diagram and write a definition of the given angle pair. (p. 31).

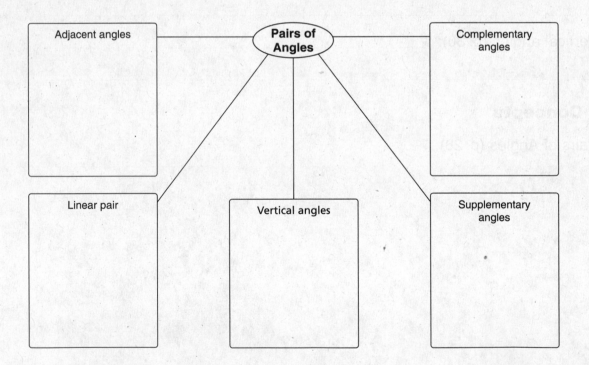

Geometry

Using Formulas in Geometry

Lesson Objectives (p. 36):

_____

_____

Vocabulary

1. Perimeter (p. 36): _____

_____

2. Area (p. 36): _____

_____

3. Base (p. 36): _____

_____

4. Height (p. 36): _____

_____

5. Diameter (p. 37): _____

_____

6. Radius (p. 37): _____

_____

7. Circumference (p. 37): _____

_____

8. Pi (p. 37): _____

_____

Key Concepts

9. Perimeter and Area (p. 36):

RECTANGLE	SQUARE	TRIANGLE

Geometry

10. Circumference and Area of a Circle (p. 37):

11. Get Organized In each shape, write the formula for its area and perimeter. (p. 37).

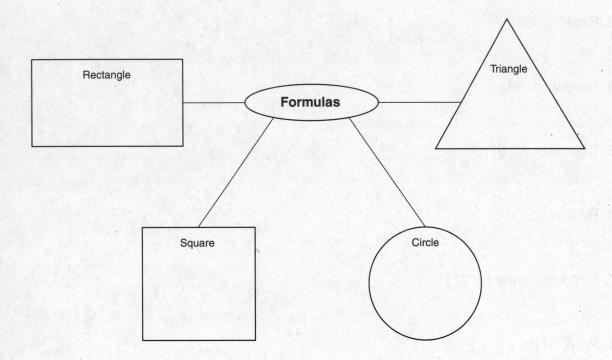

Geometry

Midpoint and Distance in the Coordinate Plane

Know it! Note

Lesson Objectives (p. 43):

_____

_____

Vocabulary

1. Coordinate plane (p. 43): _____

_____

2. Leg (p. 45): _____

_____

3. Hypotenuse (p. 45): _____

_____

Key Concepts

4. Midpoint Formula (p. 43):

5. Distance Formula (p. 44):

Geometry

6. Pythagorean Theorem (p. 45):

7. Get Organized In each box, write a formula and make a sketch that illustrates the formula. (p. 46).

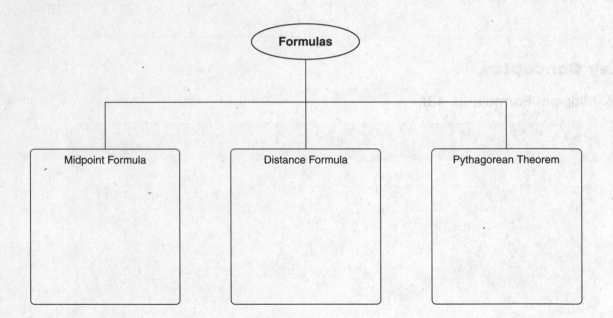

Geometry

Transformations in the Coordinate Plane

Lesson Objectives (p. 50):

_____

_____

_____

Vocabulary

1. Transformation (p. 50): _____

_____

_____

2. Preimage (p. 50): _____

_____

3. Image (p. 50): _____

_____

4. Reflection (p. 50): _____

_____

5. Rotation (p. 50): _____

_____

6. Translation (p. 50): _____

_____

_____

Geometry

Key Concepts

7. Transformations (p. 50):

Reflection	Rotation	Translation

8. Get Organized In each box, sketch an example of each transformation. (p. 52).

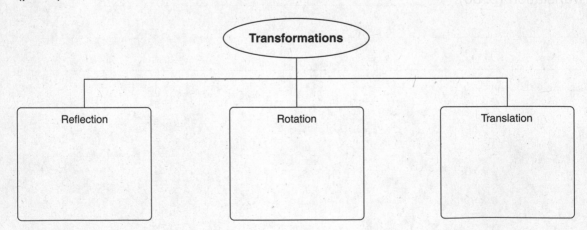

Geometry

Chapter Review

1-1 Understanding Points, Lines, and Planes

Draw and label each of the following.

1. a segment containing the points A and B

2. a ray with endpoint M that passes through N

3. a plane containing a line segment with endpoints X and Y

4. three coplanar lines intersecting in one point.

Name each of the following.

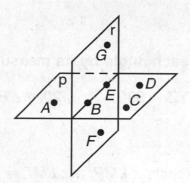

5. three coplanar points

6. a line contained in neither plane

7. a segment contained in plane R

8. a line contained in both planes

1-2 Measuring and Constructing Segments

Find the length of each segment.

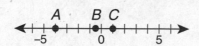

9. $\overline{AB}$

10. $\overline{BC}$

11. $\overline{AC}$

12. Sketch, draw, and construct a segment congruent to $\overline{EF}$.

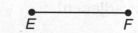

Geometry

13. *B* is between *A* and *C*. *AC* = 24 and *BC* = 11. Find *AB*.

14. *Y* is between *X* and *Z*. Find *XY*.

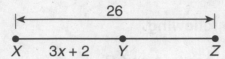

M is the midpoint of $\overline{AB}$. *AM* = 9*x* − 6, and *BM* = 6*x* + 27.

15. Find *x*.

16. Find *AM*.

17. Find *BM*.

1-3 Measuring and Constructing Angles

18. Name all the angles in the diagram.

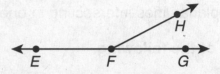

Classify each angle by its measure.

19. m∠*XYZ* = 89°

20. m∠*PQR* = 150°

21. m∠*BRZ* = 90°

22. $\overrightarrow{MT}$ bisects ∠*LMP*, m∠*LMT*, = (3*x* + 12)°, and m∠*TMP*, = (6*x* − 24)°. Find m∠*LMP*.

23. Use a protractor and a straightedge to draw an 80° angle. Then bisect the angle.

1-4 Pairs of Angles

Tell whether the angles are only adjacent, adjacent and form a linear pair, or not adjacent.

24. ∠2 and ∠3

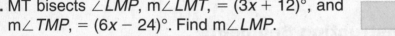

25. ∠3 and ∠4

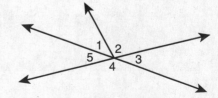

Geometry

26. $\angle 3$ and $\angle 1$

If $m\angle A = (7x - 12)°$, find the measure of each of the following.

27. supplement of $\angle A$

28. complement of $\angle A$

1-5 Using Formulas in Geometry

Find the perimeter and area of each figure.

29.
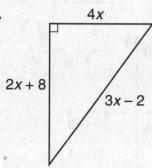

30.
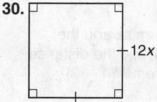

31.
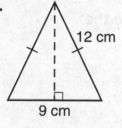

32.
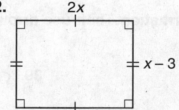

33. Find the circumference and area of a circle with radius 9 in. Use the π key on your calculator and round to the nearest tenth.

1-6 Midpoint and Distance in the Coordinate Plane

34. Find the coordinates of the midpoint of $\overline{AB}$ with endpoints $A(-2, 6)$, and $B(-4, -1)$.

Geometry

35. S is the midpoint of $\overline{RT}$, R has coordinates $(-4, -3)$ and S has coordinates $(3, 5)$. Find the coordinates of T.

36. Using the distance formula, find PQ and RS to the nearest tenth. Then determine if $\overline{PQ} \cong \overline{RS}$.

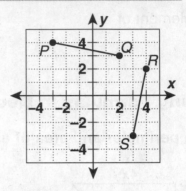

37. Using the Distance Formula and the Pythagorean Theorem, find the distance, to the nearest tenth, from $M(4, -3)$ to $N(-5, 2)$.

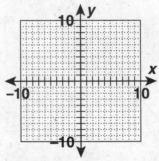

1-7 Transformations in the Coordinate Plane

Identify the transformation. Then use arrow notation to describe the transformation.

38.

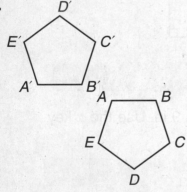

39.

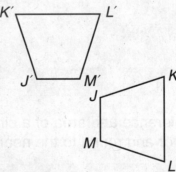

Geometry

40. Find the coordinates for the image of figure *JKLM* after the translation $(x, y) \rightarrow (x - 1, y + 2)$. Graph the image.

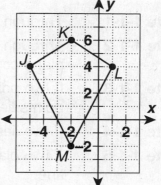

41. A figure has vertices at $A(2, 4)$, $B(-5, 1)$ and $C(0, -3)$. After a transformation, the image of the figure has vertices at $A'(5, 6)$, $B'(-2, 3)$, and $C'(3, -1)$. Graph the preimage and image. Then, identify the transformation.

Postulates and Theorems

Postulate 1-1-1	Through any two points there is exactly one line.
Postulate 1-1-2	Through any three noncollinear points there is exactly one plane containing them.
Postulate 1-1-3	If two points lie in a plane, then the line containing those points lies in the plane.
Postulate 1-1-4	If two lies intersect, then they intersect in exactly one point.
Postulate 1-1-5	If two planes intersect, then they intersect in exactly one line.
Postulate 1-2-1	(Ruler Postulate) The points on a line can be put into a one-to-one correspondence with the real numbers.
Postulate 1-2-2	(Segment Addition Postulate) If B is between A and C, then $AB + BC = AC$.
Postulate 1-3-1	(Protractor Postulate) Given $\overleftrightarrow{AB}$ and a point O on $\overleftrightarrow{AB}$, all rays that can be drawn from O can be put into a one-to-one correspondence with the real numbers from 0 to 180.
Postulate 1-3-2	(Angle Addition Postulate) If S is in the interior of $\angle PQR$, then $m\angle PQS + m\angle SQR = m\angle PQR$.

Geometry

Answer these questions to summarize the important concepts from Chapter 1 in your own words.

1. What are the building blocks of geometric figures?

2. How are angles classified? Give an example of each.

3. How are the Distance formula and the Pythagorean Theorem related to one another?

4. What the different types of transformations?

For more review of Chapter 1:

• Complete the Chapter 1 Study Guide and Review on pages 60–63 of your textbook.

• Complete the Ready to Go On quizzes on pages 35 and 59 of your textbook.

Geometry

The table contains important vocabulary terms from Chapter 2. As you work through the chapter, fill in the page number, definition, and a clarifying example.

Term	Page	Definition	Clarifying Example
biconditional statement			
conclusion			
conditional statement			
conjecture			
contrapositive			
counterexample			
deductive reasoning			
hypothesis			

Geometry

Term	Page	Definition	Clarifying Example
inductive reasoning			
logically equivalent statements			
negation			
polygon			
quadrilateral			
theorem			
triangle			
truth value			

Geometry

Using Inductive Reasoning to Make Conjectures

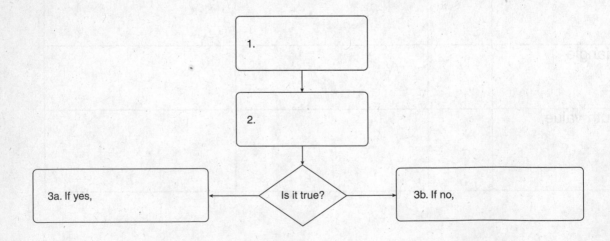

Lesson Objectives (p. 74):

_____

_____

Vocabulary

1. Inductive Reasoning (p. 74): _____

_____

2. Conjecture (p. 74): _____

_____

3. Counterexample (p. 75): _____

_____

Key Concepts

4. Inductive Reasoning (p. 75):

5. Get Organized In each box, describe the steps of the inductive reasoning process. (p. 76).

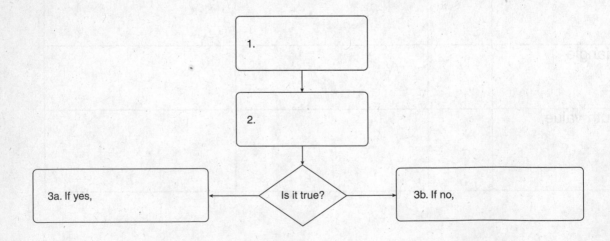

1.

2.

3a. If yes,   Is it true?   3b. If no,

Geometry

Conditional Statements

Lesson Objectives (p. 81):

_____

_____

Vocabulary

1. Conditional statement (p. 81): _____

_____

2. Hypothesis (p. 81): _____

_____

3. Conclusion (p. 81): _____

_____

4. Truth value (p. 82): _____

_____

5. Negation (p. 82): _____

_____

6. Converse (p. 83): _____

_____

7. Inverse (p. 83): _____

_____

8. Contrapositive (p. 83): _____

_____

9. Logically equivalent statements (p. 83): ____

_____

Geometry

Key Concepts

10. Conditional Statements (p. 81):

DEFINITION	SYMBOLS	VENN DIAGRAM

11. Related Conditionals (p. 83):

DEFINITION	SYMBOLS

12. Get Organized In each box, write the definition and give an example. (p. 84).

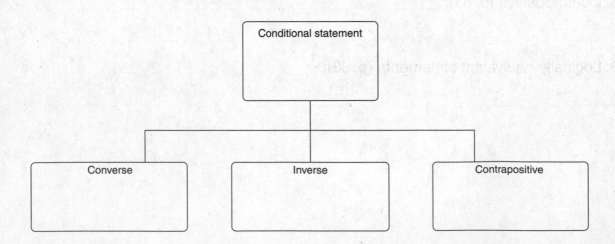

Geometry

Using Deductive Reasoning to Verify Conjectures

Lesson Objectives (p. 88):

_____

_____

Vocabulary

1. Deductive Reasoning (p. 88): _____

_____

Key Concepts

2. Law of Detachment (p. 89):

3. Law of Syllogism (p. 89):

4. Get Organized Write each law in your own words and give an example of each. (p. 90).

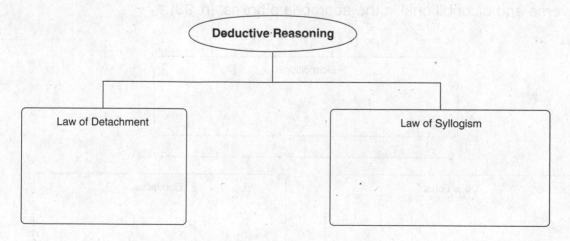

Deductive Reasoning

Law of Detachment   Law of Syllogism

Geometry

Biconditional Statements and Definitions

Lesson Objectives (p. 96):

_____

_____

Vocabulary

1. Biconditional statement (p. 96): _____

_____

2. Definition (p. 97): _____

_____

3. Polygon (p. 98): _____

_____

_____

4. Triangle (p. 98): _____

_____

5. Quadrilateral (p. 98): _____

_____

Key Concepts

6. Get Organized Use the definition of a polygon to write a conditional, converse and biconditional in the appropriate boxes. (p. 98).

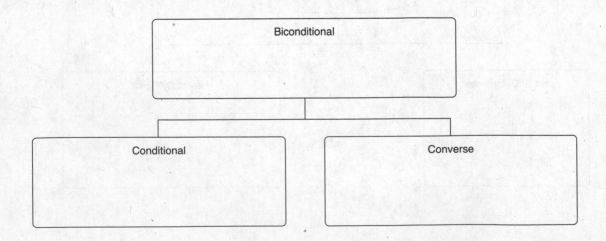

Geometry

Algebraic Proof

Lesson Objectives (p. 104):

_____

_____

_____

Vocabulary

1. Proof (p. 104): _____

_____

_____

Key Concepts

2. Properties of Equality (p. 104):

Addition Property of Equality	
Subtraction Property of Equality	
Multiplication Property of Equality	
Division Property of Equality	
Reflexive Property of Equality	
Symmetric Property of Equality	
Transitive Property of Equality	
Substitution Property of Equality	

Geometry

3. Properties of Congruence (p. 106):

SYMBOLS	EXAMPLE
Reflexive Property of Congruence	
Symmetric Property of Congruence	
Transitive Property of Congruence	

4. Get Organized In each box, write an example of the property, using the correct symbol. (p. 107).

Property	Equality	Congruence
Reflexive		
Symmetric		
Transitive		

Geometry

Geometric Proof

Lesson Objectives (p. 110):

_____

_____

Vocabulary

1. Theorem (p. 110): _____

2. Two-column proof (p. 111): _____

_____

_____

Key Concepts

3. Theorem 2-6-1—Linear Pair (p. 110):

THEOREM	HYPOTHESIS	CONCLUSION
2-6-1 Linear Pair Theorem		

4. Theorem 2-6-2—Congruent Supplements (p. 111):

THEOREM	HYPOTHESIS	CONCLUSION
2-6-2 Congruent Supplements Theorem		

Geometry

5. Theorems (p. 112):

THEOREM	HYPOTHESIS	CONCLUSION
2-6-3 Right Angle Congruence Theorem		
2-6-4 Congruent Complements Theorem		

6. The Proof Process (p.112):

The Proof Process

7. Get Organized In each box, describe the steps of the proof process. (p.113).

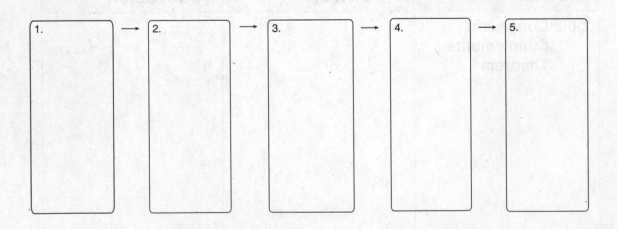

Geometry

Flowchart and Paragraph Proofs

Lesson Objectives (p. 118):

_____

_____

Vocabulary

1. Flowchart proof (p. 118): _____

_____

2. Paragraph proof (p. 120): _____

_____

Key Concepts

3. Theorem 2-7-1—Common Segments (p. 118):

THEOREM	HYPOTHESIS	CONCLUSION

4. Theorems (p. 120):

THEOREM	HYPOTHESIS	CONCLUSION
2-7-2 Vertical Angles Theorem		
2-7-3		

Geometry

5. Get Organized In each box, describe the proof style in your own words.
(p. 122)

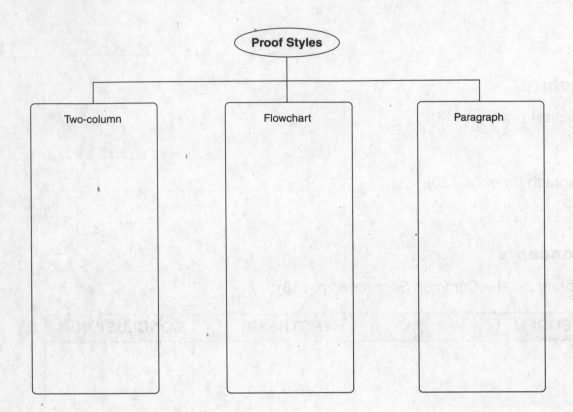

2-1 Using Inductive Reasoning to Make Conjectures

Find the next term in each pattern.

1. 6, 12, 18, . . .

2. January, April, July, . . .

3. The table shows the score on a reaction time test given to five students in both the morning and afternoon. The lower scores indicate a faster reaction time. Use the table to make a conjecture about reaction times.

Student	Morning	Afternoon
Ann	2.4	1.9
Betsy	3.1	2.7
Carla	4.0	3.9
Denise	2.7	2.8
Ellen	2.2	2.0

4. Show that the conjecture "If a number is a multiple of 5, then it is an odd number" is false by finding a counterexample.

2-2 Conditional Statements

5. Identify the hypothesis and conclusion of the conditional statement "Two angles whose sum is 90° are complementary angles".

Write a conditional statement from each of the following.

6.

Integers
Even Numbers

7. An angle that measures 90° is a right angle.

Geometry

Determine if each conditional is true. If false, give a counterexample.

8. If an angle has a measure of 90°, then it is an acute angle.

9. If $6x - 2 = 4x + 12$, then $x = 3$.

10. Write the converse, inverse, and contrapositive of the statement "If a number is divisible by 4, then it is an even number." Find the truth value of each.

converse:
truth value:
inverse:

truth value:
contrapositive:

truth value:

2-3 Using Deductive Reasoning to Verify Conjectures

11. Determine if the following conjecture is valid by the Law of Detachment.
Given: Nicholas can watch 30 minutes of television if he cleans his room first. Nicholas cleans his room.
Conjecture: Nicholas watches 30 minutes of television.

12. Determine if the following conjecture is valid by the Law of Syllogism.
Given: If a point A is on $\overline{MN}$, then it divides $\overline{MN}$ into $\overline{MA}$ and $\overline{AN}$. If $\overline{MA} \cong \overline{AN}$ then A is the midpoint of $\overline{MN}$.
Conjecture: If a point is on $\overline{MN}$, then A is the midpoint of $\overline{MN}$.

2-4 Biconditional Statements and Definitions

13. For the conditional "If two angles are complementary, then the sum of the measures is 90°," write the converse and a biconditional statement.

Converse:

Biconditional statement:

Geometry

14. Determine if the biconditional "A point divides a segment into two congruent segments if and only if the point is the midpoint of the segment," is true. If false, give a counterexample.

2-5 Algebraic Proof

Solve each equation. Write a justification for each step.

15. $m + 3 = -2$　　　　**16.** $3m - 4 = 20$　　　　**17.** $\frac{x}{-2} = -5$

Identify the property that justifies each statement.

18. $m\angle 1 \cong m\angle 2$, so $m\angle 1 + m\angle 3 = m\angle 2 = m\angle 3$

19. $\overline{MN} \cong \overline{PQ}$, so $\overline{PQ} \cong \overline{MN}$

20. $AB = CD$ and $CD = EF$, so $AB = EF$

21. $m\angle A = m\angle A$

2-6 Geometric Proof

22. Fill in the blanks to complete the two-column proof.

Given: $m\angle MOP = m\angle ROP = 90°$
$\angle 1 \cong \angle 4$

Prove: $\angle 2 \cong \angle 3$

Proof:

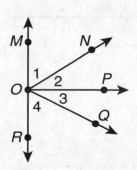

Geometry

Statements	Reasons
1.	1. Given
2. $m\angle 1 = m\angle 4$	2.
3. $m\angle 1 + m\angle 2 = m\angle MOP$ $m\angle 3 + m\angle 4 = m\angle MOP$	3.
4.	4. Transitive Property of Equality
5. $m\angle 1 + m\angle 2 = m\angle 3 + m\angle 1$	5.
6.	6. Subtraction Property of Equality

23. Use the given plan to write a
two-column proof.

Given: $\angle MOP \cong \angle NOQ$

Prove: $\angle MON = \angle POQ$

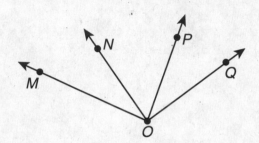

Plan: By the definition of angle
congruence, $m\angle MOP = m\angle NOQ$.
Use the angle addition postulate to show that $m\angle MOP = m\angle MON +$
$m\angle NOP$. Show a similar statement for $\angle NOQ$. Use the given fact to equate
$m\angle MON + m\angle NOP$ and $m\angle POQ + m\angle NOP$. The subtraction property of
equality allows you to show $m\angle MON = m\angle POQ$. Use the definition of
congruent triangles to establish what needs to be proved.

Statements	Reasons

Geometry

2-7 Flowchart and Paragraph Proofs

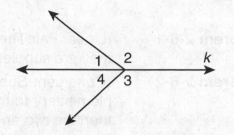

Use the given two-column proof to write the following.

Given: $\angle 1 \cong \angle 4$
Prove: $\angle 1$ is supplementary to $\angle 3$

Statements	Reasons
1. $\angle 1 \cong \angle 4$	1. Given
2. $m\angle 1 = m\angle 4$	2. Definition of Congruent Angles
3. $\angle 1$ & $\angle 2$ are supplementary. $\angle 3$ & $\angle 4$ are supplementary.	3. Linear Pair Theorem
4. $m\angle 1 + m\angle 2 = 180°$ $m\angle 3 + m\angle 4 = 180°$	4. Definition of Supplementary Angles
5. $m\angle 1 + m\angle 2 = m\angle 3 + m\angle 4$	5. Transitive Property of Equality
6. $m\angle 1 + m\angle 2 = m\angle 3 + m\angle 1$	6. Substitution Property of Equality
7. $m\angle 2 = m\angle 3$	7. Subtraction Property of Equality
8. $m\angle 1 + m\angle 3 = 180°$	8. Substitution Property of Equality
9. $\angle 1$ is supplementary to $\angle 3$.	9. Definition of Supplementary $\angle$s

24. a flowchart proof

25. a paragraph proof

Geometry

Theorem 2-6-1   (Linear Pair Theorem) If two angles form a linear pair, then they are supplementary.

Theorem 2-6-2   (Congruent Supplements Theorem) If two angles are supplementary to the same angle (or to two congruent angles), then the two angles are congruent.

Theorem 2-6-3   (Right Angle Congruence Theorem) All right angles are congruent.

Theorem 2-6-4   (Congruent Complements Theorem) If two angles are complementary to the same angle (or to two congruent angles), then the two angles are congruent.

Theorem 2-7-1   (Common Segments Theorem) If $\overline{AB} \cong \overline{CD}$, then $\overline{AC} \cong \overline{BD}$.

Theorem 2-7-2   (Vertical Angles Theorem) Vertical angles are congruent.

Theorem 2-7-3   If two congruent angles are supplementary, then each angle is a right angle.

Geometry

Answer these questions to summarize the important concepts from Chapter 2 in your own words.

1. Explain how to verify whether a conjecture is true or false.

2. Explain the difference between the hypothesis and conclusion of a conditional statement.

3. What is a biconditional statement?

4. Explain the different types of geometric proofs.

For more review of Chapter 2:

• Complete the Chapter 2 Study Guide and Review on pages 130–133 of your textbook.

• Complete the Ready to Go On quizzes on pages 103 and 127 of your textbook.

Geometry

Vocabulary

The table contains important vocabulary terms from Chapter 3. As you work through the chapter, fill in the page number, definition, and a clarifying example.

Term	Page	Definition	Clarifying Example
alternate exterior angles			
alternate interior angles			
distance from a point to a line			
parallel lines			
parallel planes			
perpendicular lines			
point-slope form			

Geometry

Term	Page	Definition	Clarifying Example
rise			
run			
same-side interior angles			
skew lines			
slope			
slope-intercept form			
transversal			

Geometry

Lines and Angles

Lesson Objectives (p. 146):

_____

_____

Vocabulary

1. Parallel lines (p. 146): _____

_____

2. Perpendicular lines (p. 146): _____

_____

3. Skew lines (p. 146): _____

_____

4. Parallel planes (p. 146): _____

_____

5. Transversal (p. 147): _____

_____

6. Corresponding angles (p. 147): _____

_____

7. Alternate interior angles (p. 147): _____

_____

8. Alternate exterior angles (p. 147): _____

_____

9. Same-side interior angles (p. 147): _____

_____

Geometry

Key Concepts

10. Parallel, Perpendicular, and Skew Lines (p. 146):

Parallel lines	
Perpendicular lines	
Skew lines	
Parallel planes	

11. Angle Pairs Formed by a Transversal (p. 147):

TERM	EXAMPLE

Geometry

12. Get Organized In each box, list all the angle pairs of each type in the diagram. (p. 148).

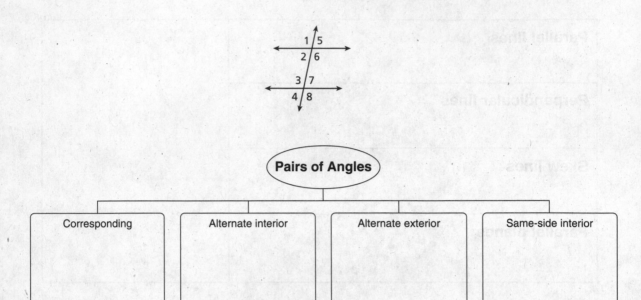

Angles Formed by Parallel Lines and Transversals

Lesson Objectives (p. 155):

_____

_____

Key Concepts

1. Postulate 3-2-1—Corresponding Angles Postulate (p. 155):

THEOREM	HYPOTHESIS	CONCLUSION

2. Theorems—Parallel Lines and Angle Pairs (p. 156):

THEOREM	HYPOTHESIS	CONCLUSION
3-2-2 Alternate Interior Angles Theorem		
3-2-3 Alternate Exterior Angles Theorem		
3-2-4 Same-Side Interior Angles Theorem		

Geometry

3. Get Organized Complete the graphic organizer by explaining why each of the three theorems is true. (p. 157).

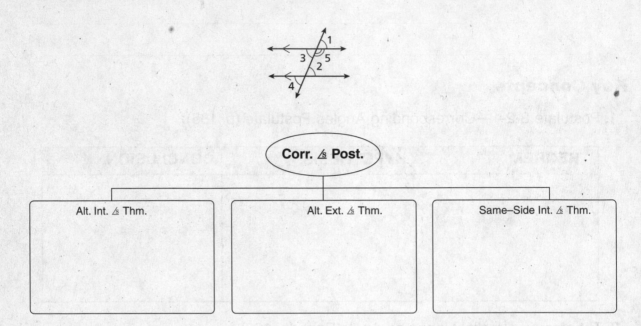

Corr. ∠ Post.

Alt. Int. ∠ Thm.	Alt. Ext. ∠ Thm.	Same–Side Int. ∠ Thm.

Geometry

Proving Lines Parallel

Lesson Objectives (p. 162):

_____

_____

Key Concepts

1. Postulate 3-3-1—Converse of the Corresponding Angles Postulate (p. 162):

THEOREM	HYPOTHESIS	CONCLUSION

2. Postulate 3-3-2—Parallel Postulate (p. 163):

Geometry

3. Theorems—Proving Lines Parallel (p. 163):

THEOREM	HYPOTHESIS	CONCLUSION
3-3-3 Converse of the Alternate Interior Angles Theorem		
3-3-4 Converse of the Alternate Exterior Angles Theorem		
3-3-5 Converse of the Same-side Interior Angles Theorem		

Geometry

4. Get Organized Compare the Corresponding Angles Postulate with the Converse of the Corresponding Angles Postulate. (p. 165).

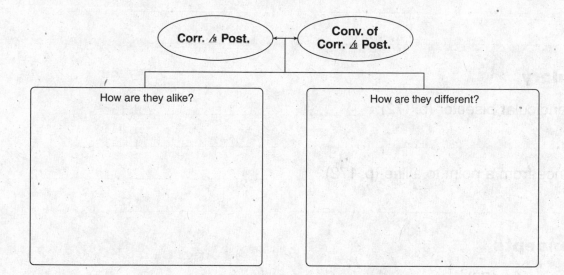

Perpendicular Lines

Lesson Objectives (p. 172):

_____

_____

Vocabulary

1. Perpendicular bisector (p. 172): _____

_____

2. Distance from a point to a line (p. 172): _____

_____

Key Concepts

3. Theorems (p. 173):

THEOREM	DIAGRAM	EXAMPLE
3-4-1		
3-4-2 Perpendicular Transversal Theorem		
3-4-3		

Geometry

4. Get Organized Use the diagram and the theorems from this lesson to complete the table. (p. 174)..

DIAGRAM	If you are given. . .	Then you can conclude. . .
	$m\angle 1 = m\angle 2$	
	$m\angle 2 = 90°$ $m\angle 3 = 90°$	
	$m\angle 2 = 90°$ $m \parallel n$	

Geometry

Slopes of Lines

Lesson Objectives (p. 182):

_____

_____

Vocabulary

1. Rise (p. 182): _____

_____

2. Run (p. 182): _____

_____

3. Slope (p. 182): _____

_____

Key Concepts

4. Slope of a Line (p. 182):

DEFINITION	EXAMPLE

5. Slopes of Parallel and Perpendicular Lines (p. 184):

3-5-1 Parallel Lines Theorem
3-5-2 Perpendicular Lines Theorem

6. Get Organized Complete the graphic organizer. (p. 185).

PAIRS OF LINES		
TYPE	**SLOPES**	**EXAMPLE**
Parallel		
Perpendicular		

Geometry

Lines in the Coordinate Plane

Lesson Objectives (p. 190):

_____

_____

Vocabulary

1. Point-slope form (p. 190): _____

_____

2. Slope-intercept form (p. 190): _____

_____

Key Concepts

3. Forms of the Equation of a Line (p. 190):

FORM	EXAMPLE

Geometry

4. Pairs of Lines (p. 192):

PARALLEL LINES	INTERSECTING LINES	COINCIDING LINES

5. Get Organized Complete the graphic organizer. (p. 193).

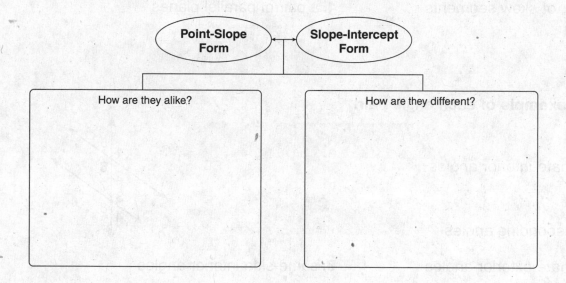

Chapter Review

3-1 Lines and Angles

Identify each of the following.

1. a pair of parallel segments

2. a pair of perpendicular segments

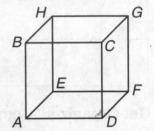

3. a pair of skew segments

4. a pair of parallel planes

Give an example of each angle pair.

5. alternate interior angles

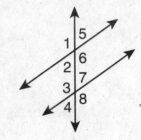

6. corresponding angles

7. alternate exterior angles

8. same-side interior angles

3-2 Angles Formed by Parallel Lines and Transversals

Find each angle measure.

9.

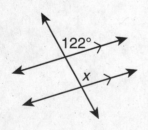

10.

(3x − 13)

(2x + 31)

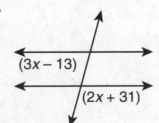

11.

(7x + 42)

(5x + 66)

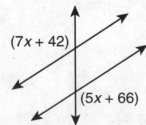

Geometry

3-3 Proving Lines Parallel

Use the given information and the theorems and postulates you have learned to show that a ‖ b.

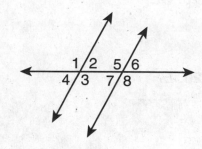

12. $m\angle 2 = m\angle 7$

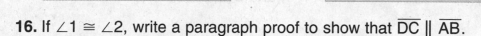

13. $m\angle 3 \times m\angle 7 = 180°$

14. $m\angle 4 = (4x + 34)°$,
$m\angle 7 = (7x - 38)°$, $x = 24$

15. $m\angle 1 \cong m\angle 5$

16. If $\angle 1 \cong \angle 2$, write a paragraph proof to show that $\overline{DC} \parallel \overline{AB}$.

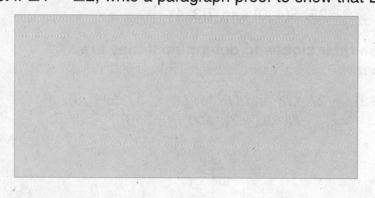

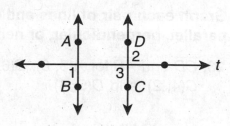

3-4 Perpendicular Lines

17. Complete the two-column proof below.

Given: $r \perp v$, $\angle 1 \cong \angle 2$

Prove: $r \perp s$

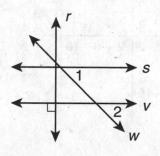

Statements	Reasons
1. $r \perp v$, $\angle 1 \cong \angle 2$	1. Given
2. $s \parallel v$	2.
3. $r \perp s$	3.

Geometry

3-5 Slopes of Lines

Use the slope formula to determine the slope of each line.

18. $\overleftrightarrow{CE}$

19. $\overleftrightarrow{AB}$

20. $\overleftrightarrow{EF}$

21. $\overleftrightarrow{DB}$

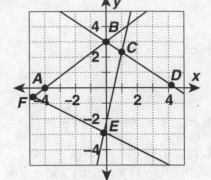

Find the slope of the line through the given points.

22. $R(2, 3)$ and $S(4, 9)$

23. $C(4, 6)$ and $D(8, 3)$

24. $H(-8, 7)$ and $I(2, 7)$

25. $S(4, 0)$ and $T(3, 4)$

Graph each pair of lines and use their slopes to determine if they are parallel, perpendicular, or neither.

26. $\overleftrightarrow{CD}$ and $\overleftrightarrow{AB}$ for $A(3, 6)$, $B(6, 12)$, $C(4, 2)$, and $D(5, 4)$

27. $\overleftrightarrow{LM}$ and $\overleftrightarrow{NP}$ for $L(-6, 1)$, $M(1, 8)$, $N(-1, -2)$, and $P(-3, 0)$

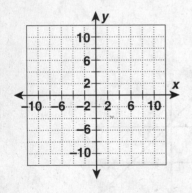

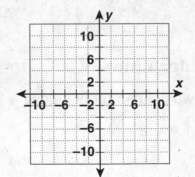

Geometry

28. $\overleftrightarrow{PS}$ and $\overleftrightarrow{RS}$ for $P(6, 6)$, $Q(5, 7)$, $R(5, -2)$, and $S(7, 2)$

29. $\overleftrightarrow{GH}$ and $\overleftrightarrow{FJ}$ for $F(-5, -4)$, $G(-3, -10)$, $H(-5, 0)$, and $J(-8, -1)$

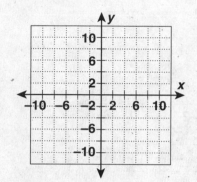

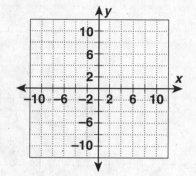

3-6 Lines in the Coordinate Plane

Write the equation of each line in the given form.

30. the line through $(1, -1)$ and $(-3, -3)$ in slope-intercept form

31. the line through $(-5, -6)$ with slope $\frac{2}{5}$ in point-slope form

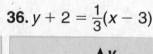

32. the line with y-intercept 3 through the point $(4, 1)$ in slope-intercept form

33. the line with x-intercept 5 and y-intercept -2 in slope-intercept form

Graph each line.

34. $y = -3x + 2$ **35.** $x = 4$ **36.** $y + 2 = \frac{1}{3}(x - 3)$

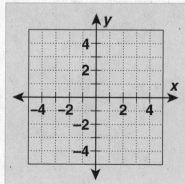

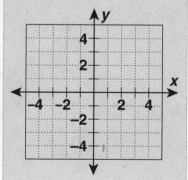

Geometry

Write the equation of each line.

37.

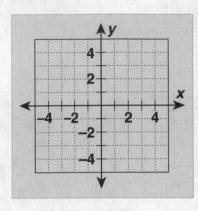

38.

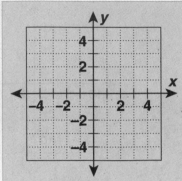

39.

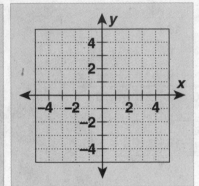

Determine whether the lines are parallel, intersect, or coincide.

40.
$$4x + 5y = 10$$
$$y = -\frac{4}{5}x + 2$$

41.
$$y = -7x + 1$$
$$y = -7x - 3$$

42.
$$y = 6x - 5$$
$$4x + 6y = 8$$

Geometry

Postulates and Theorems

Postulate 3-2-1	(Corresponding Angles Postulate) If two parallel lines are cut by a transversal, then the pair of corresponding angles are congruent.
Theorem 3-2-2	(Alternate Interior Angles Theorem) If two parallel lines are cut by a transversal, then the pairs of alternate interior angles are congruent.
Theorem 3-2-3	(Alternate Exterior Angles Theorem) If two parallel lines are cut by a transversal, the two pairs of alternate exterior angles are congruent.
Theorem 3-2-4	(Same-Side Interior Angles Theorem) If two parallel lines are cut by a transversal, then the two pairs of same-side interior angles are supplementary.
Postulate 3-3-1	(Converse of the Corresponding Angles Postulate) If two coplanar lines are cut by a transversal so that the pair of corresponding angles are congruent, then the two lines are parallel.
Postulate 3-3-2	(Parallel Postulate) Through a point P not on line l, there is exactly one line parallel to l.
Theorem 3-3-3	(Converse of the Alternate Interior Angles Theorem) If two coplanar lines are cut by a transversal so that a pair of alternate interior angles are congruent, then the two lines are parallel.
Theorem 3-3-4	(Converse of the Alternate Exterior Angles Theorem) If two coplanar lines are cut by a transversal so that a pair of alternate exterior angles are congruent, then the two lines are parallel.
Theorem 3-3-5	(Converse of the Same-Side Interior Angles Theorem) If two coplanar lines are cut by a transversal so that a pair of same-side interior angles are supplementary, then the two lines are parallel.
Theorem 3-4-1	If two intersecting lines form a linear pair of congruent angles, then the lines are perpendicular.
Theorem 3-4-2	(Perpendicular Transversal Theorem) In a plane, if a transversal is perpendicular to one of two parallel lines, then it is perpendicular to the other line.
Theorem 3-4-3	If two coplanar lines are perpendicular to the same line, then the two lines are parallel.

Geometry

Theorem 3-5-1   (Parallel Lines Theorem) In a coordinate plane, two nonvertical lines are parallel if and only if they have the same slope. Any two vertical lines are parallel.

Theorem 3-5-2   (Perpendicular Lines Theorem) In a coordinate plane, two nonvertical lines are perpendicular if and only if the product of their slopes is -1. Vertical and horizontal lines are perpendicular.

Geometry

Answer these questions to summarize the important concepts from Chapter 3 in your own words.

1. Explain the types of angles formed by two coplanar lines and a transversal.

2. Explain slope and how to find it in the coordinate plane.

3. Using slope explain how you can determine if two lines are parallel or perpendicular.

4. Explain one way to graph a line.

For more review of Chapter 3:

- Complete the Chapter 3 Study Guide and Review on pages 202–205 of your textbook.

- Complete the Ready to Go On quizzes on pages 181 and 201 of your textbook.

Geometry

The table contains important vocabulary terms from Chapter 4. As you work through the chapter, fill in the page number, definition, and a clarifying example.

Term	Page	Definition	Clarifying Example
acute triangle			
auxiliary line			
base of an isosceles triangle			
congruent polygons			
corresponding angles of polygons			
corresponding sides of polygons			
equiangular triangle			

Geometry

Term	Page	Definition	Clarifying Example
equilateral triangle			
exterior of a polygon			
included angle			
included side			
interior of a polygon			
isosceles triangle			
obtuse triangle			
right triangle			
vertex angle of an isosceles triangle			

Geometry

Classifying Triangles

Lesson Objectives (p. 216):

_____

_____

Vocabulary

1. Acute triangle (p. 216): _____

_____

2. Equiangular triangle (p. 216): _____

_____

3. Right triangle (p. 216): _____

_____

4. Obtuse triangle (p. 216): _____

_____

5. Equilateral triangle (p. 217): _____

_____

6. Isosceles triangle (p. 217): _____

_____

7. Scalene triangle (p. 217): _____

_____

Geometry

Key Concepts

8. Triangle Classification—By Angle Measure (p. 216):

9. Triangle Classification—By Side Lengths (p. 217):

Geometry

10. Get Organized In each box, describe each type of triangle. (p. 218).

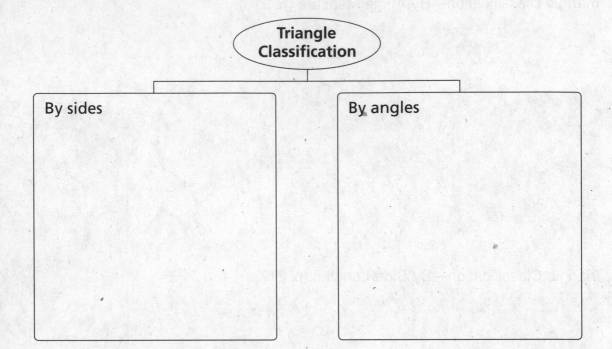

Angle Relationships in Triangles

Lesson Objectives (p. 223):

_____

_____

Vocabulary

1. Auxiliary line (p. 223): _____

_____

2. Corollary (p. 224): _____

_____

3. Interior (p. 225): _____

_____

4. Exterior (p. 225): _____

_____

5. Interior angle (p. 225): _____

_____

6. Exterior angle (p. 225): _____

_____

7. Remote interior angle (p. 225): _____

_____

Geometry

Key Concepts

8. Theorem 4-2-1—Triangle Sum Theorem (p. 223):

Theorem 4-2-1

9. Corollaries (p. 224):

Corollary	HYPOTHESIS	CONCLUSION
4-2-2		
4-2-3		

10. Theorem 4-2-4—Exterior Angle Theorem (p. 225):

Theorem 4-2-4

Geometry

11. Theorem 4-2-5—Third Angles Theorem (p. 226):

THEOREM	HYPOTHESIS	CONCLUSION

12. Get organized In each box, write each theorem in words and then draw a diagram to represent it. (p. 226).

THEOREM	WORDS	DIAGRAM
Triangle Sum Theorem		
Exterior Angle Theorem		
Third Angles Theorem		

Geometry

Congruent Triangles

Lesson Objectives (p. 231):

_____

_____

Vocabulary

1. Corresponding angles (p. 231): _____

_____

2. Corresponding sides (p. 231): _____

_____

3. Congruent polygons (p. 231): _____

_____

Key Concepts

4. Properties of Congruent Polygons (p. 231):

DIAGRAM	CORRESPONDING ANGLES	CORRESPONDING SIDES

Geometry

5. Get Organized In each box, name the congruent corresponding parts.
(p. 233).

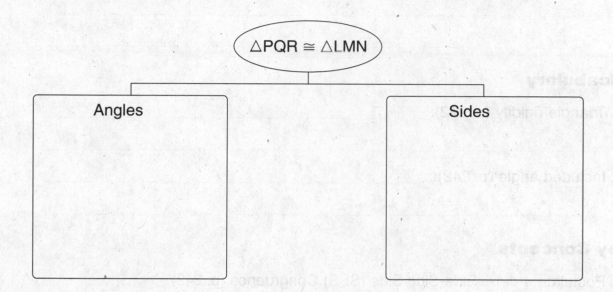

Triangle Congruence: SSS and SAS

Lesson Objectives (p. 242):

_____

_____

Vocabulary

1. Triangle rigidity (p. 242): _____

_____

2. Included angle (p. 242): _____

_____

Key Concepts

3. Postulate 4-4-1—Side-Side-Side (SSS) Congruence (p. 242)

POSTULATE	HYPOTHESIS	CONCLUSION

4. Postulate 4-4-2—Side-Angle-Side (SAS) Congruence (p. 243)

POSTULATE	HYPOTHESIS	CONCLUSION

Geometry

5. Get Organized Use the graphic organizer to compare the SSS and SAS postulates. (p. 245).

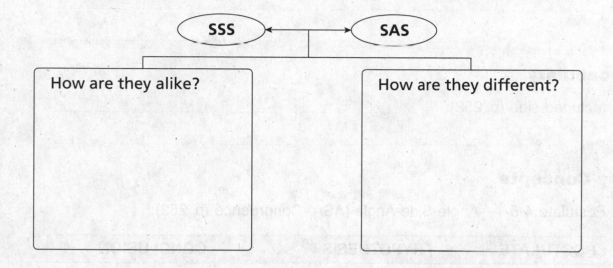

Triangle Congruence: ASA, AAS, and HL

Lesson Objectives (p. 252):

_____

_____

Vocabulary

1. Included side (p. 252): _____

_____

Key Concepts

2. Postulate 4-5-1—Angle-Side-Angle (ASA) Congruence (p. 252):

POSTULATE	HYPOTHESIS	CONCLUSION

3. Theorem 4-5-2—Angle-Angle-Side (AAS) Congruence (p. 254):

THEOREM	HYPOTHESIS	CONCLUSION

Geometry

4. Theorem 4-5-3—Hypotenuse-Leg (HL) Congruence (p. 255):

THEOREM	HYPOTHESIS	CONCLUSION

Geometry

5. Get Organized In each column, write a description of the method and then sketch two triangles, marking the appropriate congruent parts. (p. 255).

PROVING TRIANGLES CONGRUENT						
	Def. of $\triangle \cong$	SSS	SAS	ASA	AAS	HL
Words						
Pictures						

Geometry

Triangle Congruence: CPCTC

Lesson Objectives (p. 260):

_____

_____

Vocabulary

1. CPCTC (p. 260): _____

_____

Key Concepts

2. **Get organized** Write all conclusions you can make using CPCTC. (p. 262).

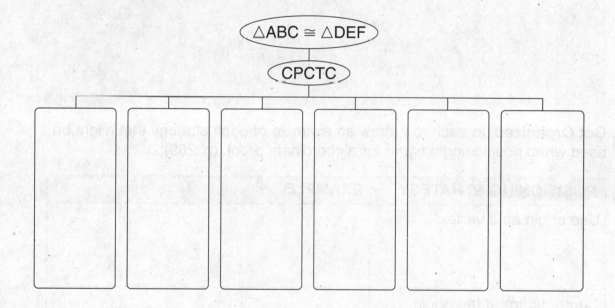

△ABC ≅ △DEF

CPCTC

Geometry

LESSON 4-7 Introduction to Coordinate Proof

Lesson Objectives (p. 267):

_____

_____

Vocabulary

1. Coordinate proof (p. 267): _____

_____

Key Concepts

2. Strategies for Positioning Figures in the Coordinate Plane (p. 267):

3. **Get Organized** In each row, draw an example of each strategy that might be used when positioning a figure for a coordinate proof. (p. 269):

POSITIONING STRATEGY	EXAMPLE
Use origin as a vertex.	
Center figure at the origin.	
Center side of figure at origin.	
Use axes as sides of figure.	

Geometry

Isosceles and Equilateral Triangles

LESSON 4-8

Lesson Objectives (p. 273):

_____

_____

Vocabulary

1. Legs of an isosceles triangle (p. 273): _____

_____

2. Vertex angle (p. 273): _____

_____

3. Base (p. 273): _____

_____

4. Base angles (p. 273): _____

_____

Key Concepts

5. Theorems—Isosceles Triangle (p. 273):

THEOREM	HYPOTHESIS	CONCLUSION
4-8-1 Isosceles Triangle Theorem		
4-8-2 Converse of Isosceles Triangle Theorem		

Geometry

6. Corollary 4-8-3—Equilateral Triangle (p. 274):

COROLLARY	HYPOTHESIS	CONCLUSION

7. Corollary 4-8-4—Equiangular Triangle (p. 275):

COROLLARY	HYPOTHESIS	CONCLUSION

8. Get Organized In each box, draw and mark a diagram for each type of triangle. (p. 276).

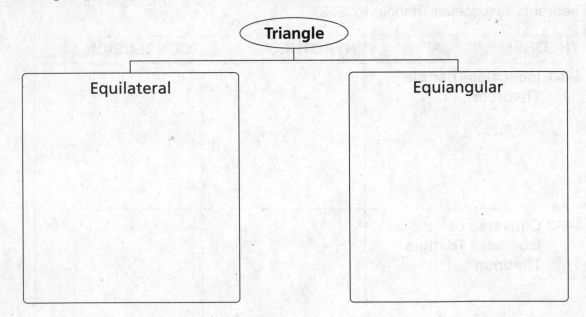

Geometry

Chapter Review

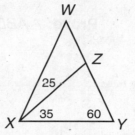

4-1 Classifying Triangles

Classify each triangle by its angle measure.

1. △XYZ

2. △XYW

3. △XZW

Classify each triangle by its side lengths.

4. △DEF

5. △DEG

6. △EFG

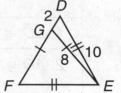

4-2 Angle Relationships in Triangles

Find each angle measure.

7. m∠ACB

8. m∠K

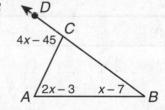

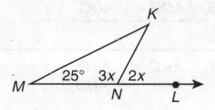

9. A carpenter built a triangular support structure
for a roof. Two of the angles of the structure
measure 32.5° and 47.5°. Find the measure
of the third angle.

4-3 Congruent Triangles

Given △ABC ≅ △XYZ. Identify the congruent corresponding parts.

10. $\overline{BC} \cong$

11. $\overline{ZX} \cong$

12. ∠A ≅

13. ∠Y ≅

Given △JKL ≅ △PQR. Find each value.

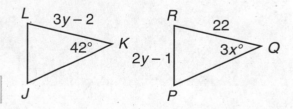

14. x

15. RP

Geometry

16. Given: $\ell \parallel k$; $\overline{BD} \cong \overline{CD}$; $\overline{AB} \cong \overline{AC}$; $\overline{AD} \perp \overline{CB}$; $\overline{AD} \perp \overline{XW}$; $\angle XAC \cong WAB$

Prove: $\triangle ABD \cong \triangle ACD$

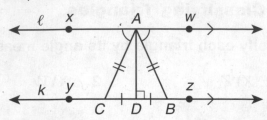

Statements	Reasons
1. $\overline{BD} \cong \overline{CD}$; $\overline{AB} \cong \overline{AC}$;	1.
2. $\overline{AD} \cong \overline{AD}$	2.
3. $\ell \parallel k$; $\overline{AD} \perp \overline{CB}$; $\overline{AD} \perp \overline{XW}$	3.
4.	4. Def. of $\perp$ lines
5. $\angle ADB \cong \angle ADC$	5.
6.	6. Given
7. $\angle XAC \cong \angle ACD$; $\angle WAB \cong \angle ABD$	7.
8.	8. Transitive Property of Congruence
9. $\angle CAD \cong \angle BAD$	9.
10.	10. Def of Congruent Triangles

4-4 Triangle Congruence: SSS and SAS

17. Given that *HIJK* is a rhombus, use SSS to explain why $\triangle HIL \cong \triangle JKL$.

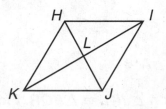

Geometry

18. Given: $\overline{NR} \cong \overline{PR}$; $\overline{MR} \cong \overline{QR}$

Prove: $\triangle MNR \cong \triangle QPR$

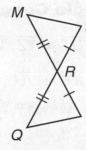

4-5 Triangle Congruence: ASA, AAS, and HL

Determine if you can use the HL Congruence Theorem to prove the triangles congruent. If not, tell what else you need to know.

19. $\triangle HIK \cong \triangle JIK$

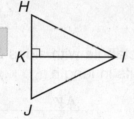

20. $\triangle PQR \cong \triangle RSP$

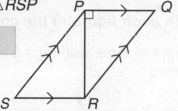

21. Use ASA to prove the triangles congruent.

Given: $\overline{BD}$ bisects $\angle ABC$ and $\angle ADC$

Prove: $\triangle ABD \cong \triangle CBD$

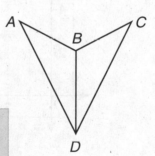

Geometry

4-6 Triangle Congruence: CPCTC

22. Given: $\overline{UZ} \cong \overline{YZ}$, $\overline{VZ} \cong \overline{XZ}$

Prove: $\overline{XY} \cong \overline{VU}$

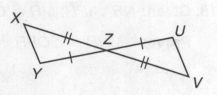

4-7 Introduction to Coordinate Proof

Position each figure in the coordinate plane.

23. a right triangle with legs 3 and 4 units in length

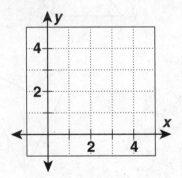

24. a rectangle with sides 6 and 8 units in length

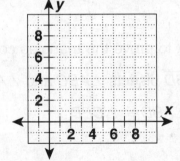

Geometry

4-8 Isosceles and Equilateral Triangles

25. Assign coordinates to each vertex and write a coordinate proof.

Given: rectangle *ABCD* with diagonals intersecting at *z*

Prove: $\overline{CZ} \cong \overline{DZ}$

Find each angle measure.

26. $m\angle B$

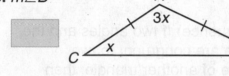

27. $m\angle HEF$

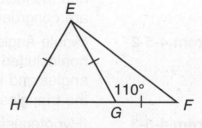

28. Given: $\triangle PQR$ has coordinates $P(0, 0)$, $Q(2a, 0)$, and $R(a, a\sqrt{3})$

Prove: $\triangle PQR$ is equilateral.

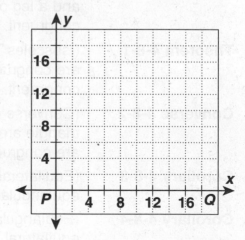

Geometry

Theorem 4-2-1	(Triangle Sum Theorem) The sum of the angle measures of a triangle is 180°. $m\angle A + m\angle B + m\angle C = 180°$
Corollary 4-2-2	The acute angles of a right triangle are complementary.
Corollary 4-2-3	The measure of each angle of an equilateral triangle is 60°.
Theorem 4-2-4	(Exterior Angle Theorem) The measure on an exterior angle of a triangle is equal to the sum of the measures of its remote interior angles.
Theorem 4-2-5	(Third Angles Theorem) If two angles of one triangle are congruent to two angles of another triangle, then the third pair of angles are congruent.
Postulate 4-4-1	(Side-Side-Side (SSS) Congruence) If three sides of one triangle are congruent to three sides of another triangle, then the triangles are congruent.
Postulate 4-4-2	(Side-Angle-Side (SAS) Congruence) If two sides and the included angle of one triangle are congruent to two sides and the included angle of another triangle, then the triangles are congruent.
Postulate 4-5-1	(Angle-Side-Angle (ASA) Congruence) If two angles and the included side of one triangle are congruent to two angles and the included side of another triangle, then the triangles are congruent.
Theorem 4-5-2	(Angle-Angle-Side (AAS) Congruence) If two angles and the nonincluded side of one triangle are congruent to two angles and the nonincluded side of another triangle, then the triangles are congruent.
Theorem 4-5-3	(Hypotenuse-Leg (HL) Congruence) If the hypotenuse and a leg of a right triangle are congruent to the hypotenuse and a leg of another right triangle, then the triangles are congruent.
Theorem 4-8-1	(Isosceles Triangle Theorem) If two sides of a triangle are congruent, then the angles opposite the sides are congruent.
Converse 4-8-2	(Converse of Isosceles Triangle Theorem) If two sides of a triangle are congruent, then the angles opposite the sides are congruent.
Corollary 4-8-3	(Equilateral Triangle) If a triangle is equilateral, then it is equiangular.
Corollary 4-8-4	(Equiangular Triangle) If a triangle is equiangular, then it is equilateral.

Geometry

Answer these questions to summarize the important concepts from Chapter 4 in your own words.

1. Name 5 ways to prove triangles congruent.

2. What do the letters CPCTC stand for?

3. Explain the relationship between the lengths of the sides of a triangle and the angles opposite of the sides of a triangle.

4. What two formulas are most useful in coordinate proofs?

For more review of Chapter 4:

• Complete the Chapter 4 Study Guide and Review on pages 284–287 of your textbook.

• Complete the Ready to Go On quizzes on pages 239 and 281 of your textbook.

Geometry

Vocabulary

The table contains important vocabulary terms from Chapter 5. As you work through the chapter, fill in the page number, definition, and a clarifying example.

Term	Page	Definition	Clarifying Example
altitude of a triangle			
centroid of a triangle			
circumcenter of a triangle			
circumscribed circle			
concurrent			
equidistant			
incenter of a triangle			

Geometry

Term	Page	Definition	Clarifying Example
inscribed circle			
locus			
median of a triangle			
midsegment of a triangle			
orthocenter of a triangle			
point of concurrency			
Pythagorean triple			

Geometry

Perpendicular and Angle Bisectors

Lesson Objectives (p. 300):

_____

_____

Vocabulary

1. Equidistant (p. 300): _____

_____

2. Locus (p. 300): _____

_____

Key Concepts

3. Theorems—Distance and Perpendicular Bisectors (p. 300):

THEOREM	HYPOTHESIS	CONCLUSION
5-1-1 Perpendicular Bisector Theorem		
5-1-2 Converse of the Perpendicular Bisector Theorem		

Geometry

4. Theorems—Distance and Angle Bisectors (p. 301):

THEOREM	HYPOTHESIS	CONCLUSION
5-1-3 Angle Bisector Theorem		
5-1-4 Converse of the Angle Bisector Theorem		

5. Get Organized In each box, write the theorem or its converse in your own words. (p. 303).

```
      ⊥ Bisector                    ∠ Bisector
  ┌──────────┬──────────┐      ┌──────────┬──────────┐
  │ Theorem  │ Converse │      │ Theorem  │ Converse │
  │          │          │      │          │          │
  │          │          │      │          │          │
  │          │          │      │          │          │
  │          │          │      │          │          │
  │          │          │      │          │          │
  └──────────┴──────────┘      └──────────┴──────────┘
```

Geometry

Bisectors of Triangles

Lesson Objectives (p. 307):

_____

_____

Vocabulary

1. Concurrent (p. 307): _____

_____

2. Point of concurrency (p. 307): _____

_____

3. Circumcenter of a triangle (p. 307): _____

_____

4. Circumscribed (p. 308): _____

_____

5. Incenter of a triangle (p. 309): _____

_____

6. Inscribed (p. 309): _____

_____

Key Concepts

7. Theorem 5-2-1—Circumcenter Theorem (p. 307):

Theorem 5-2-1

8. Theorem 5-2-2—Incenter Theorem (p. 309):

> Theorem 5-2-2

9. Get Organized Fill in the blanks to make each statement true. (p. 310).

	CIRCUMCENTER	INCENTER
Definition	The point of concurrency of the _____	The point of concurrency of the _____
Distance	Equidistant from the _____	Equidistant from the _____
Location (Inside, Outside, or On)	Can be _____ _____ the triangle?	_____ the triangle?

Geometry

Medians and Altitudes of Triangles

Lesson Objectives (p. 314):

_____

_____

Vocabulary

1. Median of a triangle (p. 314): _____

_____

2. Centroid of a triangle (p. 314): _____

_____

3. Altitude of a triangle (p. 316): _____

_____

4. Orthocenter of a triangle (p. 316): _____

_____

Key Concepts

5. Theorem 5-3-1—Centroid Theorem (p. 314):

Theorem 5-3-1

6. Get Organized In the cells sketch, measure, and name an example of each angle type. (p. 317).

	CENTROID	ORTHOCENTER
Definition	The point of concurrency of the _____	The point of concurrency of the _____
Location (Inside, Outside, or On)	_____ the triangle	Can be _____ _____ the triangle.

The Triangle Midsegment Theorem

Lesson Objectives (p. 322):

_____

_____

Vocabulary

1. Midsegment of a triangle (p. 322): _____

_____

Key Concepts

2. Theorem 5-4-1—Triangle Midsegment Theorem (p. 323):

Theorem 5-4-1

3. Get Organized Write the definition of a triangle midsegment and list its properties. Then draw an example and a nonexample. (p. 324).

Definition	Properties
Triangle Midsegment	
Example	Nonexample

Indirect Proof and Inequalities in One Triangle

Lesson Objectives (p. 332):

_____

_____

Vocabulary

1. Indirect proof (p. 332): _____

_____

Key Concepts

2. Theorems—Angle-Side Relationships in Triangles (p. 333):

THEOREM	HYPOTHESIS	CONCLUSION
5-5-1		
5-5-2		

3. Theorem 5-5-3—Triangle Inequality Theorem (p. 334):

Theorem 5-5-3

Geometry

4. Get Organized In each box, explain what you know about △*ABC* as a result of the theorem. (p. 335).

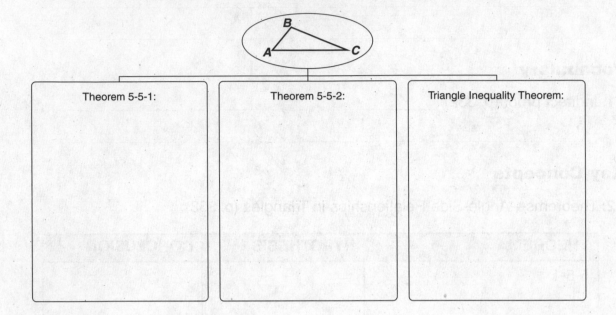

Theorem 5-5-1:	Theorem 5-5-2:	Triangle Inequality Theorem:

Geometry

Inequalities in Two Triangles

Lesson Objectives (p. 340):

_____

_____

Key Concepts

1. Theorems—Inequalities in Two Triangles (p. 340):

THEOREM	HYPOTHESIS	CONCLUSION
5-6-1 Hinge Theorem		
5-6-2 Converse of the Hinge Theorem		

Geometry

2. Get Organized In each box, use the given triangles to write a statement for the theorem. (p. 342).

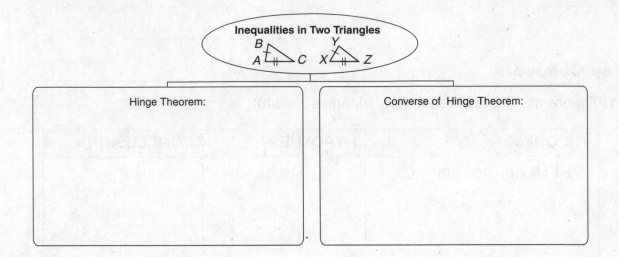

Inequalities in Two Triangles

Hinge Theorem:

Converse of Hinge Theorem:

The Pythagorean Theorem

LESSON 5-7

Lesson Objectives (p. 348):

_____

_____

Vocabulary

1. Pythagorean triple (p. 349): _____

_____

Key Concepts

2. Theorem 5-7-1—Converse of the Pythagorean Theorem (p. 350):

THEOREM	HYPOTHESIS	CONCLUSION
5-7-1		

3. Theorem 5-7-2—Pythagorean Inequalities Theorem (p. 351):

Theorem 5-7-2

Geometry

4. Get Organized In each box, summarize the Pythagorean relationship.
(p. 352).

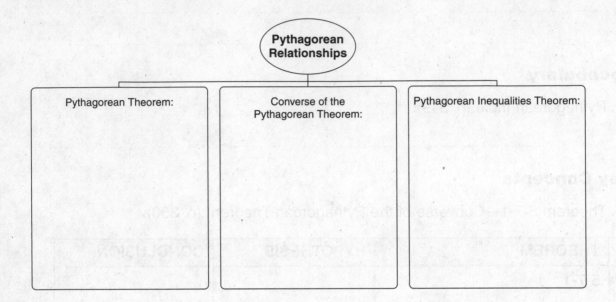

Applying Special Right Triangles

Lesson Objectives (p. 356):

_____

_____

Key Concepts

1. Theorem 5-8-1—45°-45°-90° Triangle Theorem (p. 356):

> Theorem 5-8-1

2. Theorem 5-8-2—30°-60°-90° Triangle Theorem (p. 358):

> Theorem 5-8-2

Geometry

4. Get Organized In each box, sketch the special right triangle and label its side lengths in terms of *s*. (p. 359).

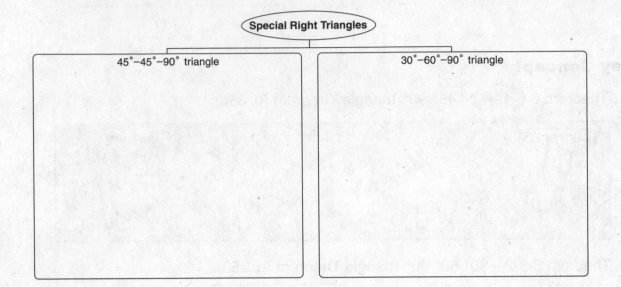

116
Geometry

5-1 Perpendicular and Angle Bisectors

Find each measure.

1. BC

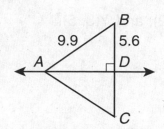

2. RS

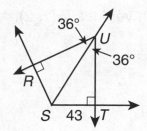

3. XW

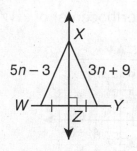

4. Write an equation in point-slope form for the perpendicular bisector of the segment with endpoints K(10, 3) and L(−2, −5).

5-2 Bisectors of Triangles

5. $\overline{NP}$, $\overline{OP}$, $\overline{MP}$ are the perpendicular bisectors of △JKL. Find PK and JM.

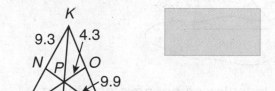

6. $\overline{DH}$ and $\overline{DG}$ are angle bisectors of △EGH. Find m∠EHD and the distance from D to $\overline{GH}$.

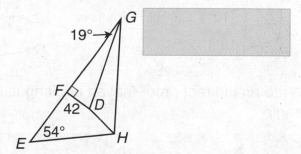

7. Find the circumcenter of △JKL with vertices J(0, 6), K(8, 0) and L(0, 0).

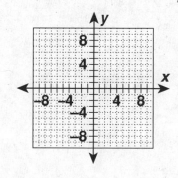

5-3 Medians and Altitudes of Triangles

8. Nathan cuts a triangle with vertices at coordinates (0, 4), (6, 0), and (3, −2) from a piece of grid paper. At what coordinates should he place the tip of a pen to balance the triangle?

9. Find the orthocenter of △WYX with vertices W(1, 2), X(7, 2), and Y(3, 5).

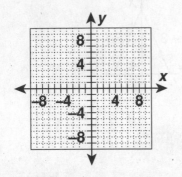

5-4 The Triangle Midsegment Theorem

10. Find BA, JC, and m∠FBA in △KCJ.

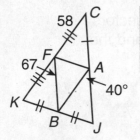

11. What is the distance MP across the lake?

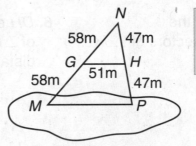

12. Write an indirect proof that an equiangular triangle can not have an obtuse angle.

Geometry

5-5 Indirect Proof and Inequalities in One Triangle

13. Write the angles of △QRS in order from smallest to largest.

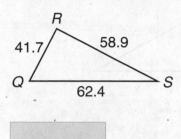

14. Write the sides of △ABC in order from shortest to longest.

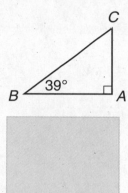

Tell whether a triangle can have sides with given lengths. Explain.

15. 7.7, 9.4, 16.1

16. $3r$, $r + 4$, r^2 when $r = 5$

17. The distance from Tyler's house to the library is 3 miles. The distance from his home to the park is 12 miles. If the three locations form a triangle, what is the range of distance from the library to the park?

5-6 Inequalities in Two Triangles

18. Compare *KL* and *NP*.

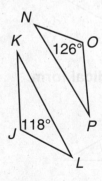

19. Compare $m\angle BAD$ and $m\angle CAD$.

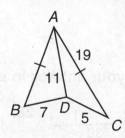

20. Find the range of values of x.

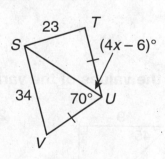

Geometry

5-7 The Pythagorean Theorem

21. Find the value of *x*. Give the answer in simplest radical form.

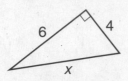

22. Find the missing side length. Tell if the side lengths form a Pythagorean. Explain.

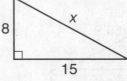

23. Tell if the measures 9, 40, and 41 can be the side lengths of a triangle. If so, classify the triangle as acute, obtuse or right.

24. A carpenter wants to cut a rectangular piece of wood. He checks to see if the diagonal measurements are the same. What should they measure?

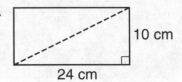

10 cm

24 cm

5-8 Applying Special Right Triangles

25. A flag is an equilateral triangle with the side length of 24 inches. What is the height *h* of the flag? Round your answer to the nearest inch.

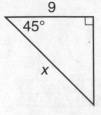

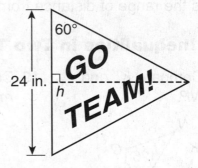

60°

GO TEAM!

24 in.

h

Find the values of the variables. Give your answer in simplest radical form.

26.

9

45°

x

x

27.

12

30°

x

y

28.

14

60°

x

y

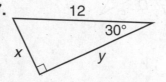

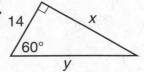

Geometry

Theorem 5-1-1	(Perpendicular Bisector Theorem) If a point is on the perpendicular bisector of a segment, then it is equidistant from the endpoints of the segment.
Converse 5-1-2	(Converse of the Perpendicular Bisector Theorem) If a point is equidistant from the endpoints of a segment, then it is on the perpendicular bisector of the segment.
Theorem 5-1-3	(Angle Bisector Theorem) If a point is on the bisector of an angle, then it is equidistant from the sides of the angle.
Converse 5-1-4	(Converse of the Angle Bisector Theorem) If a point in the interior of an angle is equidistant from the sides of the angle, then it is on the bisector of the angle.
Theorem 5-2-1	(Circumcenter Theorem) The circumcenter of a triangle is equidistant from the vertices of the triangle.
Theorem 5-2-2	(Incenter Theorem) The incenter of a triangle is equidistant from the sides of the triangle.
Theorem 5-3-1	(Centroid Theorem) The centroid of a triangle is located $\frac{2}{3}$ of the distance from each vertex to the midpoint of the opposite side.
Theorem 5-4-1	(Triangle Midsegment Theorem) A midsegment of a triangle is parallel to a side of the triangle, and its length is half the length of that side.
Theorem 5-5-1	If two sides of a triangle are not congruent, then the larger angle is opposite the longer side.
Theorem 5-5-2	If two angles of a triangle are not congruent, then the longer side is opposite the larger angle.
Theorem 5-5-3	(Triangle Inequality Theorem) The sum of any two side lengths of a triangle is greater than the third side length.
Theorem 5-6-1	(Hinge Theorem) If two sides of one triangle are congruent to two sides of another triangle and the included angles are not congruent, then the longer third side is across from the larger included angle.
Converse 5-6-2	(Converse of the Hinge Theorem) If two sides of one triangle are congruent to two sides of another triangle and the third sides are not congruent, then the larger included angle is across from the longer third side.

Geometry

Theorem 5-7-1 (Converse of the Pythagorean Theorem) If the sum of the squares of the lengths of two sides of a triangle is equal to the square of the length of the third side, then the triangle is a right triangle.

Theorem 5-7-2 (Pythagorean Inequalities Theorem) In $\triangle ABC$, c is the length of the longest side.

Theorem 5-8-1 (45°-45°-90° Triangle Theorem) In a 45°-45°-90° triangle, both legs are congruent, and the length of the hypotenuse is the length of a leg times $\sqrt{2}$.

Theorem 5-8-2 (30°-60°-90° Triangle Theorem) In a 30°-60°-90° triangle, the length of the hypotenuse is 2 times the length of the shorter leg, and the length of the longer leg is the length of the shorter leg times $\sqrt{3}$.

Geometry

Big Ideas

Answer these questions to summarize the important concepts from Chapter 5 in your own words.

1. Explain the difference in location between the circumcenter and the incenter of a triangle.

2. Why is the centroid of a triangle also called the *center of gravity*?

3. Describe how many midsegments each triangle has and what is formed by them.

4. Use the Pythagorean theorem to describe an obtuse and acute triangle such as $\triangle ABC$.

For more review of Chapter 5:

- Complete the Chapter 5 Study Guide and Review on pages 366–369 of your textbook.

- Complete the Ready to Go On quizzes on pages 329 and 365 of your textbook.

Geometry

The table contains important vocabulary terms from Chapter 6. As you work through the chapter, fill in the page number, definition, and a clarifying example.

Term	Page	Definition	Clarifying Example
base angle of a trapezoid			
base of a trapezoid			
concave (polygon)			
convex (polygon)			
diagonal (of a polygon)			
isosceles trapezoid			
kite			
leg of a trapezoid			

Geometry

Term	Page	Definition	Clarifying Example
midsegment of a trapezoid			
parallelogram			
rectangle			
regular polygon			
rhombus			
side of a polygon			
square			
trapezoid			
vertex of a polygon			

Geometry

Properties and Attributes of Polygons

Lesson Objectives (p. 382):

_____

_____

Vocabulary

1. Side of a polygon (p. 382): _____

_____

2. Vertex of a polygon (p. 382): _____

_____

3. Diagonal (p. 382): _____

_____

4. Regular polygon (p. 382): _____

_____

5. Concave (p. 383): _____

_____

6. Convex (p. 383): _____

_____

Key Concepts

7. Polygons (p. 382):

NUMBER OF SIDES	NAME OF POLYGON
3	
4	
5	
6	
7	
8	
9	
10	
12	
n	

8. Polygons (p. 383):

POLYGON	NUMBER OF SIDES	NUMBER OF TRIANGLES	SUM OF INTERIOR ANGLE MEASURES
Triangle			
Quadrilateral			
Pentagon			
Hexagon			
n-gon			

Geometry

9. Theorem 6-1-1—Polygon Angle Sum Theorem (p. 383):

Theorem 6-1-1

10. Theorem 6-1-2—Polygon Exterior Angle Sum Theorem (p. 384):

Theorem 6-1-2

11. Get Organized In each cell, write the formula for finding the indicated value for a regular convex polygon with *n* sides. (p. 385).

	INTERIOR ANGLES	EXTERIOR ANGLES
Sum of Angle Measures		
One Angle Measure		

Geometry

Properties of Parallelograms

Lesson Objectives (p. 391):

_____

_____

Vocabulary

1. Parallelogram (p. 391): _____

_____

Key Concepts

2. Theorem 6-2-1—Properties of Parallelograms (p. 391):

THEOREM	HYPOTHESIS	CONCLUSION
6-2-1		

3. Theorems—Properties of Parallelograms (p. 392):

THEOREM	HYPOTHESIS	CONCLUSION
6-2-2		
6-2-3		
6-2-4		

Geometry

4. Get Organized In each cell, draw a figure with markings that represent the given property. (p. 394).

Properties of Parallelograms				
Opp. sides ‖	Opp. sides ≅	Opp. ∠s ≅	Cons. ∠s supp.	Diag. bisect each other.

Conditions for Parallelograms

Lesson Objectives (p. 398):

_____

_____

Key Concepts

1. Theorems—Conditions for Parallelograms (p. 398):

THEOREM	EXAMPLE
6-3-1	
6-3-2	
6-3-3	

2. Theorems—Conditions for Parallelograms (p. 399):

THEOREM	EXAMPLE
6-3-4	
6-3-5	

Geometry

3. Get Organized In each box, write one of the six conditions for a parallelogram. Then sketch a parallelogram and label it to show how it meets the condition. (p 401).

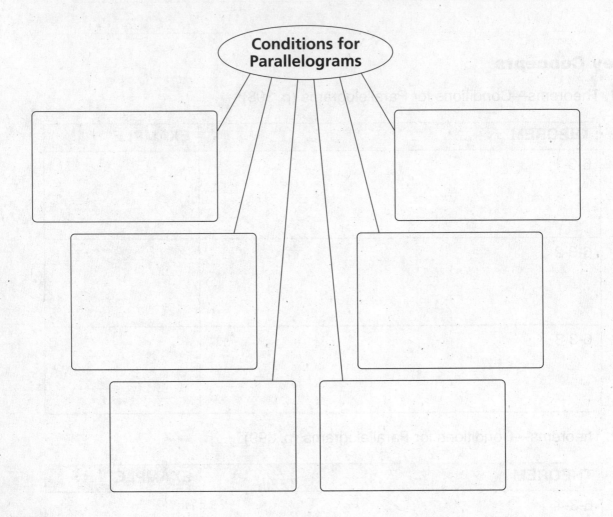

Properties of Special Parallelograms

Lesson Objectives (p. 408):

_____

_____

Vocabulary

1. Rectangle (p. 408): _____

_____

2. Rhombus (p. 409): _____

_____

3. Square (p. 410): _____

_____

_____

Key Concepts

4. Theorems—Properties of Rectangles (p. 408):

THEOREM	HYPOTHESIS	CONCLUSION
6-4-1		
6-4-2		

Geometry

4. Theorems—Properties of Rhombuses (p. 409):

THEOREM	HYPOTHESIS	CONCLUSION
6-4-3		
6-4-4		
6-4-5		

5. Get Organized Write the missing terms in the three unlabeled sections. Then write a definition of each term. (p. 411).

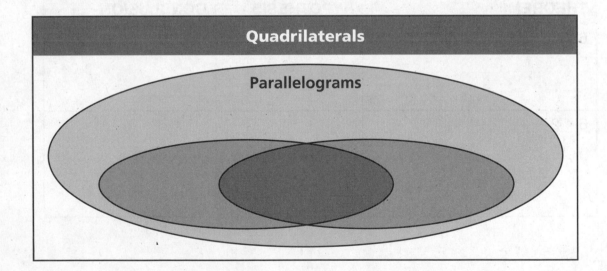

Conditions for Special Parallelograms

Lesson Objectives (p. 418):

_____

_____

Key Concepts

1. Theorems—Conditions for Rectangles (p. 418):

THEOREM	EXAMPLE
6-5-1	
6-5-2	

2. Theorems—Conditions for Rhombuses (p. 419):

THEOREM	EXAMPLE
6-5-3	
6-5-4	
6-5-5	

Geometry

3. Get Organized In each box, write at least three conditions for the given parallelogram. (p. 421).

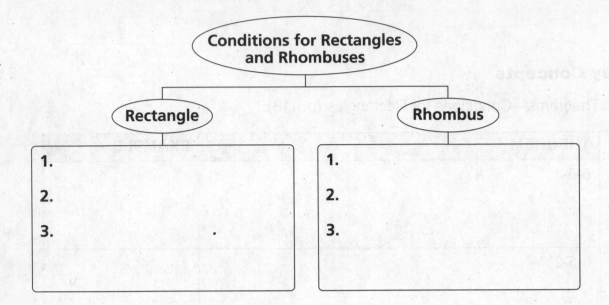

Conditions for Rectangles and Rhombuses

Rectangle
1.
2.
3.

Rhombus
1.
2.
3.

Geometry

Properties of Kites and Trapezoids

Lesson Objectives (p. 427):

_____

_____

Vocabulary

1. Kite (p. 427): _____

_____

2. Trapezoid (p. 429): _____

_____

3. Base of a trapezoid (p. 429): _____

_____

4. Leg of a trapezoid (p. 429): _____

_____

5. Base angle of a trapezoid (p. 429): _____

_____

6. Isosceles trapezoid (p. 429): _____

_____

7. Midsegment of a trapezoid (p. 431): _____

_____

Geometry

Key Concepts

8. Theorems—Properties of Kites (p. 427):

THEOREM	HYPOTHESIS	CONCLUSION
6-6-1		
6-6-2		

9. Theorems—Isosceles Trapezoids (p. 429):

THEOREM	DIAGRAM	EXAMPLE
6-6-3		
6-6-4		
6-6-5		

Geometry

10. Theorem 6-6-6—Trapezoid Midsegment Theorem (p. 431):

Theorem 6-6-6

11. Get Organized Write the missing terms in the unlabeled sections. Then write the definition of each term. (p. 431)

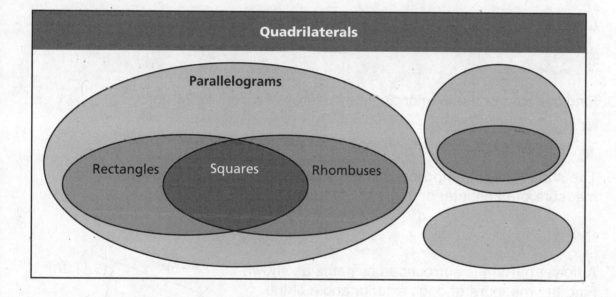

Chapter Review

6-1 Properties and Attributes of Polygons

Tell whether each figure is a polygon. If it is a polygon, name it by the number of its sides.

1.

2.

3.

4.

5. Find the sum of the interior angle measures of a convex 24-gon.

6. The surface of a trampoline is in the shape of a regular octagon. Find the measure of each interior angle of the trampoline.

7. A flower garden is surrounded by paths as shown. Find the measure of each exterior angle of the flower garden.

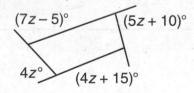

$(7z - 5)°$ $(5z + 10)°$
$4z°$ $(4z + 15)°$

8. Find the measure of each exterior angle of a regular hexagon.

Geometry

6-2 Properties of Parallelograms

In parallelogram *ABCD*, *CD* = 20, *BE* = 9, and
m∠*DAB* = 50°. Find each measure.

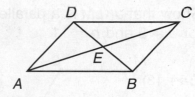

9. *BD*

10. *AB*

11. *DE*

12. m∠*ABC*

13. m∠*BCD*

14. m∠*CDA*

15. Three vertices of ▱*DEFG* are *E*(−1, −3), *F*(4, −1), and *G*(−2, 1).
Find the coordinates of vertex *D*.

PQRS is a parallelogram.
Find each measure.

16. *PS*

17. *QR*

18. m∠*P*

19. m∠*S*

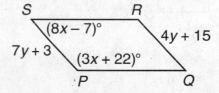

6-3 Conditions for Parallelograms

20. Show that *ABCD* is a parallelogram for
x = 3 and *y* = 9.

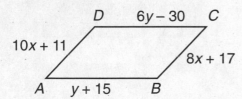

Geometry

21. Show that *JKLM* is a parallelogram for $a = 5$ and $b = 11$.

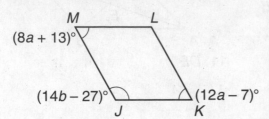

Determine if each quadrilateral must be a parallelogram. Justify your answer.

22.

23.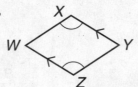

24.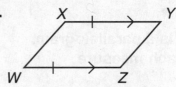

25. Show that a quadrilateral with vertices $A(-3, 6)$, $B(-5, 0)$, $C(4, 3)$ and $D(2, -3)$ is a parallelogram.

Geometry

6-4 Properties of Special Parallelograms

In rectangle *QRST*, *RT* = 55, and *QR* = 45.
Find each length.

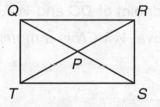

26. *PR*

27. *RS*

28. *QS*

29. *QP*

WXYZ is a rhombus. Find each measure.

30. *YZ*

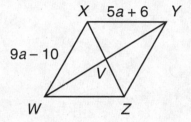

31. m∠*WXZ* and m∠*XYZ* if m∠*YVZ* = (7*b* + 27)°
and m∠*WYZ* = (3*b* + 7)°.

32. Given: *ABCD* and *WXYZ* are congruent rhombi. *M* is the midpoint of $\overline{BC}$ and $\overline{WX}$ and *N* is the midpoint of $\overline{DC}$ and $\overline{WZ}$.

Prove: *WMCN* is a rhombus.

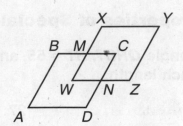

Geometry

6-5 Conditions for Special Parallelograms

Determine if the conclusion is valid. If not, tell what additional information is needed to make it valid.

33. Given: $\overline{AB} \cong \overline{CD}$; $\overline{BC} \parallel \overline{AD}$
Conclusion: *ABCD* is a parallelogram.

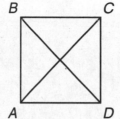

34. Given: $\overline{AC}$ bisects $\overline{BD}$.
Conclusion: *ABCD* is a rectangle.

Use the diagonals to determine whether a parallelogram with the given vertices is a rectangle, rhombus, or square. Give all the names that apply.

35. $W(-4, -1)$, $X(-1, 3)$, $Y(3, 0)$, $Z(0, -4)$

36. $M(0, 1)$, $N(2, 6)$, $P(4, 1)$, $Q(2, -4)$

Geometry

37. Given: *WXYZ* is a rhombus; *E*, *F*, *G* and *H* are midpoints; m∠*FEH* = 90°

Prove: *EFGH* is a rectangle.

6-6 Properties of Kites and Trazezoids

In kite *MNPQ*, m∠*NQP* = 70° and m∠*NMQ* = 60°. Find each measure.

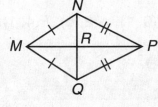

38. m∠*NMR*

39. m∠*MQR*

40. m∠*NPR*

41. m∠*MQP*

42. Find *MN*

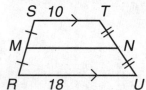

Geometry

Theorem 6-1-1	(Polygon Angle Sum Theorem) The sum of the interior angle measures of a convex polygon with n sides is $(n - 2)180°$.
Theorem 6-1-2	(Polygon Exterior Angle Sum Theorem) The sum of the exterior angle measures, one angle at each vertex, of a convex polygon is 360°.
Theorem 6-2-1	If a quadrilateral is a parallelogram, then its opposite sides are congruent.
Theorem 6-2-2	If a quadrilateral is a parallelogram, then its opposite angles are congruent.
Theorem 6-2-3	If a quadrilateral is a parallelogram, then its consecutive angles are supplementary.
Theorem 6-2-4	If a quadrilateral is a parallelogram, then its diagonals bisect each other.
Theorem 6-3-1	If one pair of opposite sides of a quadrilateral are parallel and congruent, then the quadrilateral is a parallelogram.
Theorem 6-3-2	If both pairs of opposite sides of a quadrilateral are congruent, then the quadrilateral is a parallelogram.
Theorem 6-3-3	If both pairs of opposite angles of a quadrilateral are congruent, then the quadrilateral is a parallelogram.
Theorem 6-3-4	If an angle of a quadrilateral is supplementary to both of its consecutive angles, then the quadrilateral is a parallelogram.
Theorem 6-3-5	If both pairs of opposite sides of a quadrilateral are congruent, then the quadrilateral is a parallelogram.
Theorem 6-4-1	If a quadrilateral is a rectangle, then it is a parallelogram.
Theorem 6-4-2	If a parallelogram is a rectangle, then its diagonals are congruent.
Theorem 6-4-3	If a quadrilateral is a rhombus, then it is a parallelogram.
Theorem 6-4-4	If a parallelogram is a rhombus, then its diagonals are perpendicular.
Theorem 6-4-5	If a parallelogram is a rhombus, then each diagonal bisects a pair of opposite angles.
Theorem 6-5-1	If one angle of a parallelogram is a right angle, then the parallelogram is a rectangle.

Geometry

Theorem 6-5-2	If the diagonals of a parallelogram are congruent, then the parallelogram is a rectangle.
Theorem 6-5-3	If one pair of consecutive sides of a parallelogram are congruent, then the parallelogram is a rhombus.
Theorem 6-5-4	If the diagonals of a parallelogram are perpendicular, then the parallelogram is a rhombus.
Theorem 6-5-5	If one diagonal of a parallelogram bisects a pair of opposite angles, then the parallelogram is a rhombus.
Theorem 6-6-1	If a quadrilateral is a kite, then its diagonals are perpendicular.
Theorem 6-6-2	If a quadrilateral is a kite, then exactly one pair of opposite angles are congruent.
Theorem 6-6 3	If a quadrilateral is an isosceles trapezoid, then each pair of base angles are congruent.
Theorem 6-6-4	If a trapezoid has one pair of congruent base angles, then the trapezoid is isosceles.
Theorem 6-6-5	A trapezoid is isosceles if and only if its diagonals are congruent.
Theorem 6-6-6	The midsegment of a trapezoid is parallel to each base, and its length is one half the sum of the lengths of the bases.

Geometry

Answer these questions to summarize the important concepts from Chapter 6 in your own words.

1. Name five ways to determine if a quadrilateral is a parallelogram.

2. Explain why a square is a rectangle but a rectangle is not necessarily a square.

3. Explain the difference between a rhombus and a kite.

4. Explain the difference between a regular polygon and a polygon that is not regular.

For more review of Chapter 6:

- Complete the Chapter 6 Study Guide and Review on pages 438–441 of your textbook.

- Complete the Ready to Go On quizzes on pages 407 and 437 of your textbook.

Geometry

Vocabulary

The table contains important vocabulary terms from Chapter 7. As you work through the chapter, fill in the page number, definition, and a clarifying example.

Term	Page	Definition	Clarifying Example
cross product			
dilation			
extremes of a proportion			
indirect measurement			
means of a proportion			

Geometry

Term	Page	Definition	Clarifying Example
proportion			
ratio			
scale			
scale drawing			
scale factor			
similar			
similar polygons			
similarity ratio			

Geometry

Ratio and Proportion

LESSON 7-1

Lesson Objectives (p. 454):

_____

_____

Vocabulary

1. Ratio (p. 454): _____

_____

2. Proportion (p. 455): _____

_____

3. Extremes (p. 455): _____

_____

_____

4. Means (p. 455): _____

_____

5. Cross products (p. 455): _____

_____

Key Concepts

6. Properties of Proportions (p. 455):

ALGEBRA	NUMBERS

7. Get Organized In the boxes, write the definition of a proportion, the properties of proportions, and examples and nonexamples of a proportion. (p. 457).

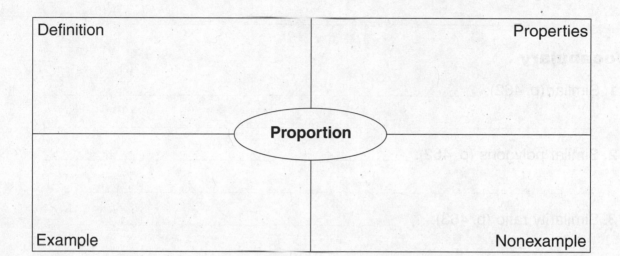

Geometry

Ratios in Similar Polygons

Lesson Objectives (p. 462):

_____

_____

Vocabulary

1. Similar (p. 462): _____

_____

2. Similar polygons (p. 462): _____

_____

3. Similarity ratio (p. 463): _____

_____

Key Concepts

4. Similar Polygons (p. 462):

DEFINITION	DIAGRAM	STATEMENTS

5. Get Organized Write the definition of similar polygons, and a similarity statement. Then draw examples and nonexamples of similar polygons. (p. 464).

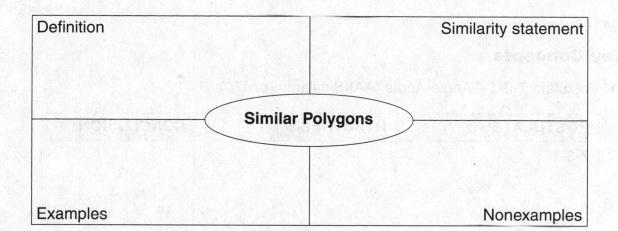

Geometry

Triangle Similarity: AA, SSS, SAS

Lesson Objectives (p. 470):

_____

_____

Key Concepts

1. Postulate 7-3-1—Angle-Angle (AA) Similarity (p. 470):

POSTULATE	HYPOTHESIS	CONCLUSION
7-3-1		

2. Theorem 7-3-2—Side-Side-Side (SSS) Similarity (p. 470):

THEOREM	HYPOTHESIS	CONCLUSION
7-3-2		

Geometry

3. Theorem 7-3-3—Side-Angle-Side (SAS) Similarity (p. 471):

THEOREM	HYPOTHESIS	CONCLUSION
7-3-3		

4. Properties of Similarity (p. 473):

PROPERTIES OF SIMILARITY
Reflexive Property of Similarity
Symmetric Property of Similarity
Transitive Property of Similarity

Geometry

5. Get Organized If possible, write a congruence or similarity theorem or postulate in each section of the table. Include a marked diagram for each. (p. 473).

	CONGRUENCE	SIMILARITY
SSS		
SAS		
AA		

Geometry

Applying Properties of Similar Triangles

Lesson Objectives (p. 481):

_____

_____

Key Concepts

1. Theorem 7-4-1—Triangle Proportionality Theorem (p. 481):

THEOREM	HYPOTHESIS	CONCLUSION
7-4-1		

2. Theorem 7-4-2—Converse of the Triangle Proportionality Theorem (p. 482):

THEOREM	HYPOTHESIS	CONCLUSION
7-4-2		

3. Corollary 7-4-3—Two-Transversal Proportionality (p. 482):

THEOREM	HYPOTHESIS	CONCLUSION
7-4-3		

Geometry

4. Theorem 7-4-4—Triangle Angle Bisector Theorem (p. 483):

THEOREM	HYPOTHESIS	CONCLUSION
7-4-4		

5. Get Organized Draw a figure for each proportionality theorem or corollary and then measure it. Use your measurements to write an if-then statement about each figure. (p. 484).

△ Proportionality Thm.	Conv. of △ Proportionality Thm.
Proportionality Theorems	
2-Transv. Proportionality Corollary	△∠ Bisector Thm.

Using Proportional Relationships

Lesson Objectives (p. 488):

_____

_____

Vocabulary

1. Indirect measurement (p. 488): _____

_____

2. Scale drawing (p. 489): _____

_____

3. Scale (p. 489): _____

_____

Key Concepts

4. Similar Triangles—Similarity, Perimeter, and Area Ratios (p. 490):

STATEMENT	RATIO

Geometry

5. Theorem 7-5-1—Proportional Perimeters and Areas Theorem (p. 490):

7-5-1

6. Get Organized Draw and measure two similar figures. Then write the ratios for similarity, perimeter, and areas. (p. 490).

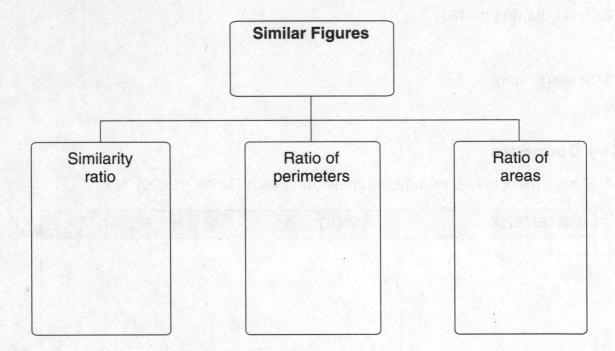

Similar Figures

| Similarity ratio | Ratio of perimeters | Ratio of areas |

Geometry

LESSON 7-6 Dilations and Similarity in the Coordinate Plane

Lesson Objectives (p. 495):

_____

_____

Vocabulary

1. Dilation (p. 495): _____

_____

2. Scale factor (p. 495): _____

_____

Key Concepts

3. Get Organized Write the definition of a dilation, a property of dilations, and an example and nonexample of a dilation. (p. 497).

Definition	Property
Example	Nonexample

Dilations

Geometry

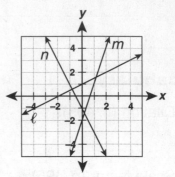

7-1 Ratio and Proportion

Write a ratio expressing the slope of each line.

1. ℓ

2. m

3. n

4. y-axis

Solve each proportion.

5. $\dfrac{x}{9} = \dfrac{16}{12}$

6. $\dfrac{8}{15} = \dfrac{20}{y}$

7. $\dfrac{6}{x+3} = \dfrac{x-3}{9}$

8. $\dfrac{3y}{10} = \dfrac{54}{5y}$

9. An architect's model for a building is 2.7 m long and 1.1 m wide. The actual building is 360 m wide. What is the length of the building?

7-2 Ratios in Similar Polygons

Determine whether the two polygons are similar. If so, write the similarity ratio and a similarity statement.

10. $\triangle ABC$ and $\triangle XYZ$

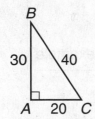 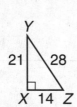

11. $\square MNOP$ and $\square RSTU$

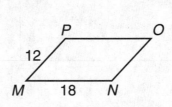 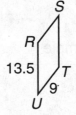

Geometry

12. Leonardo da Vinci's famous portrait of the *Mona Lisa* is 30 in. tall and 21 in. wide. *Jonathon* has a postage stamp of the *Mona Lisa* that is similar to the original painting. The height of the postage stamp is 4 cm. What is the width?

7-3 Triangle Similarity: AA, SSS, and SAS

13. Given: right $\triangle ABC$; $\overline{BD} \perp \overline{AC}$

Prove: $\triangle ABC \sim \triangle ADB$

14. Given: $\ell \parallel k$

Prove: $\triangle EFG \sim \triangle IHG$

Geometry

15. A tree stops a surveyor from directly measuring the length of a lot line. She locates points *E, F, G, H,* and *I* as shown. What is *EF*?

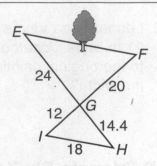

7-4 Applying Properties of Similar Triangles

Find the length of each segment.

16. $\overline{RU}$

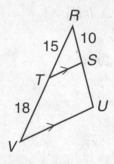

17. $\overline{BC}$

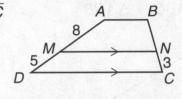

18. $\overline{FG}$ and $\overline{GH}$

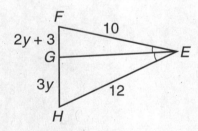

7-5 Using Proportional Relationships

The plan for an office uses the scale of 1 square:12 ft. Find the actual length of the following walls.

19. $\overline{AB}$

20. $\overline{BC}$

21. $\overline{CD}$

22. $\overline{EF}$

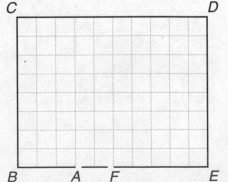

Geometry

23. A 5 ft 9 in. man cast a 6 ft 6 in. shadow. At the same time of day, a tree casts a 50 ft shadow. What is the height of the tree?

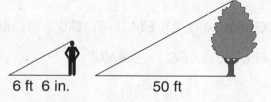

6 ft 6 in.   50 ft

7-6 Dilations and Similarity in the Coordinate Plane

24. Given: $A(-4, 4)$, $B(-2, 0)$, $C(4, 2)$, $X(-1, 3)$, $Y(0, 1)$, and $Z(3, 2)$

Prove: $\triangle ABC \sim \triangle XYZ$

Geometry

25. Given: $A(0, 4)$, $B(4, -4)$, $C(0, -4)$, $M(0, -2)$, and $N(3, -2)$

Prove: $\triangle ABC \sim \triangle ANM$

Geometry

Graph the image of each triangle after a dilation with the given scale factor. Then verify that the image is similar to the given triangle.

26. scale factor of 2

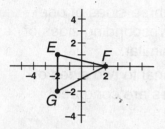

27. scale factor of $\frac{1}{2}$

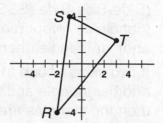

Geometry

Postulate 7-3-1	(Angle-Angle (AA) Similarity) If two angles of one triangle are congruent to two angles of another triangle, then the triangles are similar.
Theorem 7-3-2	(Side-Side-Side (SSS) Similarity) If the three sides of one triangle are proportional to the three corresponding sides of another triangle, then the triangles are similar.
Theorem 7-3-3	If two sides of one triangle are proportional to two sides of another triangle and their included angles are congruent, then the triangles are similar.
Theorem 7-4-1	(Triangle Proportionality Theorem) If a line parallel to a side of a triangle intersects the other two sides, then it divides those sides proportionally.
Theorem 7-4-2	(Converse of the Triangle Proportionality Theorem) If a line divides two sides of a triangle proportionally, then it is parallel to the third side.
Corollary 7-4-3	(Two-Transversal Proportionality) If three or more parallel lines intersect two transversals, then they divide the transversals proportionally.
Theorem 7-4-4	(Triangle Angle Bisector Theorem) An angle bisector of a triangle divides the opposite side into two segments whose lengths are proportional to the lengths of the other two sides.
Theorem 7-5-1	(Proportional Perimeters and Areas Theorem) If the similarity ratio of two similar figures is $\frac{a}{b}$, then the ratio of their perimeters is $\frac{a}{b}$, and the ratio of their areas is $\frac{a^2}{b^2}$, or $\left(\frac{a}{b}\right)^2$.

Geometry

Answer these questions to summarize the important concepts from Chapter 7 in your own words.

1. What does it mean for two triangles to be similar?

2. What is meant by the similarity ratio?

3. How can two triangles be proven similar?

4. What is the proportional perimeters and areas theorem?

For more review of Chapter 7:

- Complete the Chapter 7 Study Guide and Review on pages 504–507 of your textbook.

- Complete the Ready to Go On quizzes on pages 479 and 503 of your textbook.

Geometry

Vocabulary

The table contains important vocabulary terms from Chapter 8. As you work through the chapter, fill in the page number, definition, and a clarifying example.

Term	Page	Definition	Clarifying Example
angle of depression			
angle of elevation			
component form			
cosine			
equal vectors			
geometric mean			

Geometry

Term	Page	Definition	Clarifying Example
magnitude			
parallel vectors			
resultant vector			
sine			
tangent of an angle			
trigonometric ratio			
vector			

Geometry

Similarity in Right Triangles

Lesson Objectives (p. 518):

_____

_____

Vocabulary

1. Geometric mean (p. 519): _____

_____

_____

Key Concepts

2. Theorem 8-1-1 (p. 518):

8-1-1	

3. Corollaries—Geometric Means (p. 519):

COROLLARY	EXAMPLE	DIAGRAM
8-1-2		
8-1-3		

Geometry

4. Get Organized Label the right triangle and draw the altitude to the hypotenuse. In each box, write a proportion in which the given segment is a geometric mean. (p. 520).

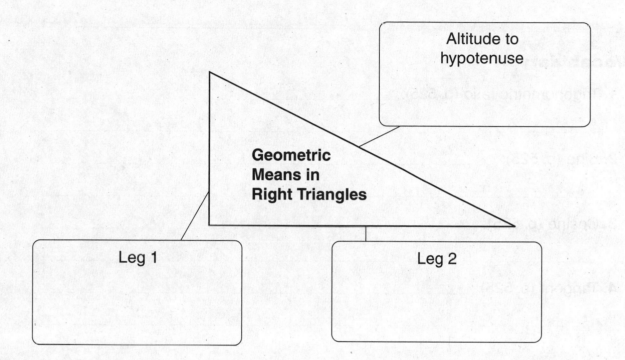

Altitude to hypotenuse

Geometric
Means in
Right Triangles

Leg 1

Leg 2

Geometry

Trigonometric Ratios

Lesson Objectives (p. 525):

_____

_____

Vocabulary

1. Trigonometric ratio (p. 525): _____

_____

2. Sine (p. 525): _____

_____

3. Cosine (p. 525): _____

_____

4. Tangent (p. 525): _____

_____

Geometry

Key Concepts

5. Trigonometric Ratios (p. 525):

DEFINITION	SYMBOLS	DIAGRAM

6. Get Organized In each cell, write the meaning of each abbreviation and draw a diagram for each. (p. 528).

ABBREVIATION	WORDS	DIAGRAM
$\sin = \dfrac{\text{opp. leg}}{\text{hyp.}}$		
$\cos = \dfrac{\text{adj. leg}}{\text{hyp.}}$		
$\tan = \dfrac{\text{opp. leg}}{\text{adj. leg}}$		

Geometry

Solving Right Triangles

Lesson Objectives (p. 534):

_____

_____

Key Concepts

1. Get Organized In each box, write a trigonometric ratio for ∠A. Then write an equivalent statement using an inverse trigonometric function. (p. 537).

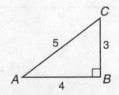

	TRIGONOMETRIC RATIO	INVERSE TRIGONOMETRIC FUNCTION
Sine		
Cosine		
Tangent		

Geometry

Angles of Elevation and Depression

Lesson Objectives (p. 544):

_____

_____

Vocabulary

1. Angle of elevation (p. 544): _____

_____

2. Angle of depression (p. 544): _____

_____

Key Concepts

3. Get Organized In each box, write a definition or make a sketch. (p. 546).

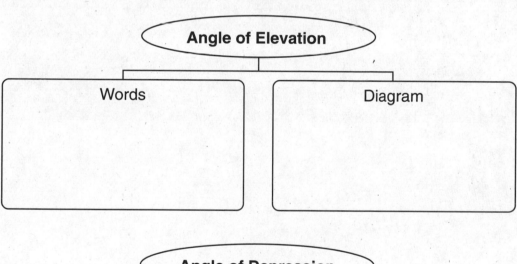

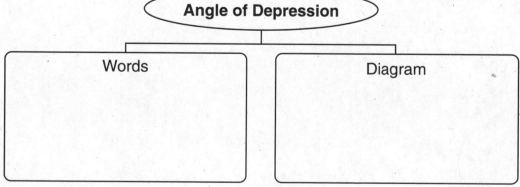

Geometry

Law of Sines and Law of Cosines

Lesson Objectives (p. 551):

_____

_____

Key Concepts

1. Theorem 8-5-1—The Law of Sines (p. 552):

> 8-5-1

2. Theorem 8-5-2—The Law of Cosines (p. 553):

> 8-5-2

Geometry

3. Get Organized Tell which law you would use to solve each given triangle and then draw an example. (p. 554).

GIVEN	LAW	EXAMPLE
Two angle measures and any side length		
Two side lengths and a nonincluded angle measure		
Two side lengths and the included angle measure		
Three side lengths		

Geometry

LESSON 8-6 Vectors

Lesson Objectives (p. 559):

_____

_____

Vocabulary

1. Vector (p. 559): _____

_____

2. Component form (p. 559): _____

_____

3. Magnitude (p. 560): _____

_____

4. Direction (p. 560): _____

_____

5. Equal vectors (p. 561): _____

_____

6. Parallel vectors (p. 561): _____

_____

7. Resultant vectors (p. 561): _____

_____

Geometry

Key Concepts

8. Vector Addition (p. 561):

METHOD	EXAMPLE
Head to Tail Method:	
Parallelogram Method:	

9. Get Organized Complete the graphic organizer. (p. 563).

Definition	Names
	Vector
Examples	Nonexamples

Geometry

8-1 Similarity in Right Triangles

Find the geometric mean of each pair of numbers. If necessary, give the answers in simplest radical form.

1. 10 and 12

2. 4.5 and 32

3. $\frac{5}{4}$ and $\frac{10}{9}$

Find *x, y,* and *z.*

4.

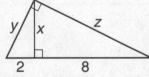

5.

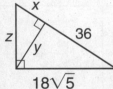

6.

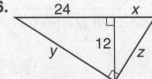

7. A surveyor needs to find the distance across a pond. What is AD to the nearest tenth of a meter?

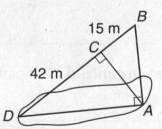

8-2 Trigonometric Ratios

Use a special right triangle to write each trigonometric ratio as a fraction.

8. tan 60°

9. cos 60°

10. sin 60°

Use your calculator to find each trigonometric ratio. Round to the nearest hundredth.

11. sin 12°

12. cos 59°

13. tan 17°

Geometry

Find each length. Round to the nearest hundredth.

14. *LK*

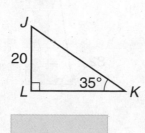

15. *AB*

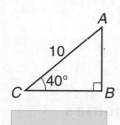

16. *WX*

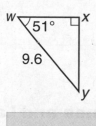

8-3 Solving Right Triangles

Find the unknown measures. Round lengths to the nearest hundredth and angle measures to the nearest degree.

17.

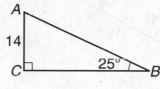

18.

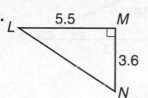

19.

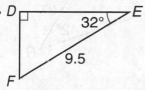

20. A bike trail has a sign warning bikers of a 7° incline for the next 12 miles. To the nearest tenth of a mile, find the vertical distance of the incline, *h*.

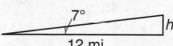

8-4 Angles of Elevation and Depression

21. From the top of a lighthouse to a ship the angle of depression is 28°. The top of the lighthouse is located 175 feet above the water. What is the horizontal distance from the lighthouse to the ship? Round to the nearest foot.

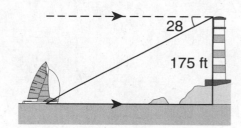

Geometry

22. The angle of elevation of the sun is 82°, a water tower casts a shadow that is 22 m long. What is the height of the water tower to the nearest tenth of a meter?

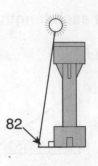

8-5 Law of Sines and Law of Cosines

Find each measure. Round lengths to the nearest tenth and angle measures to the nearest degree.

23. $m\angle P$

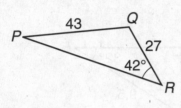

24. AB

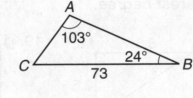

25. AC

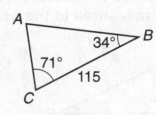

26. JL

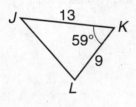

27. $m\angle A$

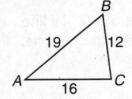

28. RP

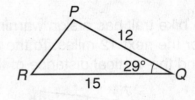

Geometry

8-6 Vectors

Draw each vector on a coordinate plane. Find its magnitude to the nearest tenth.

29. ⟨4, 1⟩

30. ⟨−3, −5⟩

31. ⟨0, 6⟩

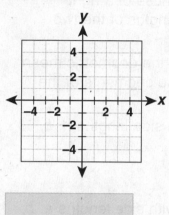

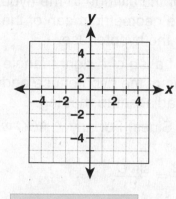

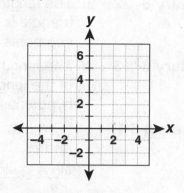

Draw each vector on a coordinate plane. Find the direction of the vector to the nearest degree.

32. A wind velocity is given by the vector ⟨2, 4⟩.

33. The path of a hiker is given by the vector ⟨7, 4⟩.

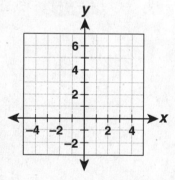

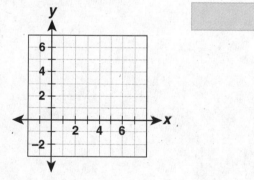

34. To reach an island, a ship leaves port and sails for 10 km at a bearing of N 48° E. It then sails due east for 14 km. What are the magnitude and direction of the voyage directly from the port to the island? Round the distance to the nearest tenth of a kilometer and the direction to the nearest degree.

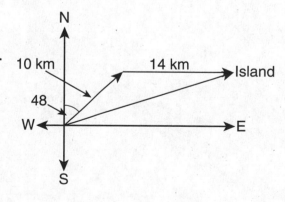

Geometry

Theorem 8-1-1 The altitude to the hypotenuse of a right triangle forms two triangles that are similar to each other and to the original triangle.

Corollary 8-1-2 The length of the altitude to the hypotenuse of a right triangle is the geometric mean of the lengths of the two segments of the hypotenuse.

Corollary 8-1-3 The length of a leg of a right triangle is the geometric mean of the lengths of the hypotenuse and the segments of the hypotenuse adjacent to that leg.

Theorem 8-5-1 (The Law of Sines) For any $\triangle ABC$ with side lengths a, b, and c,

$$\frac{\sin A}{a} = \frac{\sin B}{b} = \frac{\sin C}{c}.$$

Theorem 8-5-2 (The Law of Cosines) For any $\triangle ABC$ with side lengths a, b, and c,

$$a^2 = b^2 + c^2 - 2bc \cos A,$$
$$b^2 = a^2 + c^2 - 2ac \cos B, \text{ and}$$
$$c^2 = a^2 + b^2 - 2ab \cos C.$$

Geometry

Answer these questions to summarize the important concepts from Chapter 8 in your own words.

1. Explain the trigonometric ratios.

2. Explain what vectors are and how they are used.

3. Explain what solving a right triangle means.

4. Explain why and how the Law of Sines and Law of Cosines are used.

For more review of Chapter 8:

- Complete the Chapter 8 Study Guide and Review on pages 572–575 of your textbook.

- Complete the Ready to Go On quizzes on pages 543 and 569 of your textbook.

Geometry

Vocabulary

The table contains important vocabulary terms from Chapter 9. As you work through the chapter, fill in the page number, definition, and a clarifying example.

Term	Page	Definition	Clarifying Example
apothem			
center of a circle			
center of a regular polygon			
central angle of a regular polygon			
circle			

Geometry

Term	Page	Definition	Clarifying Example
composite figure			
geometric probability			

Geometry

Developing Formulas for Triangles and Quadrilaterals

Lesson Objectives (p. 589):

_____

_____

_____

Key Concepts

1. Postulate 9-1-1—Area Addition Postulate (p. 589):

9-1-1

2. Area—Parallelogram (p. 589):

3. Area—Triangles and Trapezoids (p. 590):

Geometry

4. Area—Rhombuses and Kites (p. 591):

5. Get Organized Name all the shapes whose area is given by each area formula and sketch an example of each shape. (p. 593).

AREA FORMULA	SHAPE(S)	EXAMPLE(S)
$A = bh$		
$A = \frac{1}{2}bh$		
$A = \frac{1}{2}(b_1 + b_2)\,h$		
$A = \frac{1}{2}d_1d_2$		

Geometry

Developing Formulas for Circles and Regular Polygons

Lesson Objectives (p. 600):

_____

_____

Vocabulary

1. Circle (p. 600): _____

_____

2. Center of a circle (p. 600): _____

_____

3. Center of a regular polygon (p. 601): _____

_____

4. Apothem (p. 601): _____

_____

5. Central angle of a regular polygon (p. 601): _____

_____

_____

Key Concepts

6. Circumference and Area—Circle (p. 600):

Geometry

7. Area—Regular Polygon (p. 601):

8. Get Organized Complete the graphic organizer. (p. 602).

REGULAR POLYGONS (SIDE LENGTH = 1)					
POLYGON	NUMBER OF SIDES	PERIMETER	CENTRAL ANGLE	APOTHEM	AREA
Triangle					
Square					
Hexagon					

Geometry

Composite Figures

Lesson Objectives (p. 606):

_____

_____

Vocabulary

1. Composite figure (p. 606): _____

_____

Key Concepts

2. **Get Organized** Complete the graphic organizer.
Use the given composite figure. (p 608).

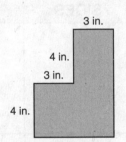

1. Divide the figure into parts.	2. Find the area of each part.	3. Add to find the total area.

Geometry

Perimeter and Area in the Coordinate Plane

Lesson Objectives (p. 616):

_____

_____

Key Concepts

1. Get Organized Complete the graphic organizer by writing the steps used to find the area of the parallelogram. (p. 619).

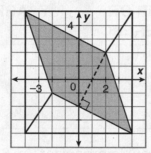

```
        ⎛                    ⎞
        ⎝  Finding the Area  ⎠
```

By using the formula:	By subtracting:

Geometry

Effects of Changing Dimensions Proportionally

Lesson Objectives (p. 622):

_____

_____

_____

Key Concepts

1. Effects of Changing Dimensions Proportionally (p. 623):

CHANGE IN DIMENSION	PERIMETER OR CIRCUMFERENCE	AREA

2. Get Organized Complete the graphic organizer. (p. 624).

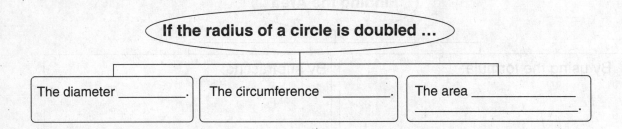

If the radius of a circle is doubled ...

The diameter _____ . The circumference _____ . The area _____ _____ .

Geometry

Geometric Probability

Lesson Objectives (p. 630):

_____

_____

Vocabulary

1. Geometric Probability (p. 630): _____

_____

Key Concepts

2. Geometric Probability (p. 630):

MODEL	LENGTH	ANGLE MEASURE	AREA
Example			
Sample Space			
Event			
Probability			

Geometry

3. Get Organized In each box, give an example of the geometric probability model. (p. 633).

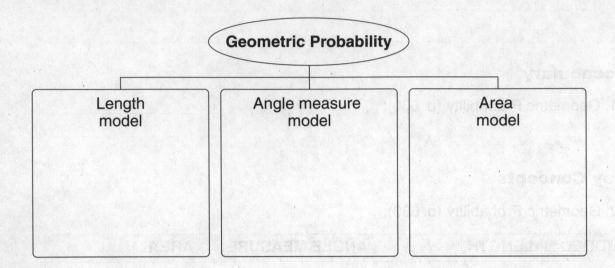

9-1 Developing Formulas for Triangles and Quadrilaterals

Find each measurement.

1. the area of the rectangle

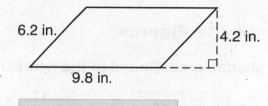

2. the area of the parallelogram

6.2 in. 4.2 in.
9.8 in.

3. the value of x when $A = 240$ ft^2

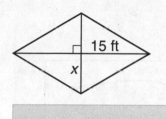

15 ft
x

4. the height of the trapezoid with $A = 110.5$ m^2

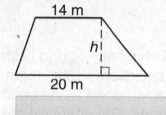

14 m
h
20 m

3. The geoboard shows a rectangle, a triangle and a trapezoid. Find the perimeter and area of each.

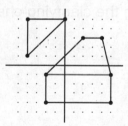

9-2 Developing Formulas for Circles and Regular Polygons

Find each measurement.

6. the circumference of $\odot C$ in terms of π

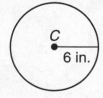

C
6 in.

7. the area of $\odot O$ in terms of π

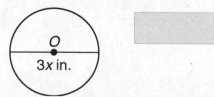

O
$3x$ in.

Geometry

Find the area of each regular polygon. Round to the nearest tenth.

8. a regular pentagon with perimeter 75 m

9. a regular octagon with apothem 8 in.

9-3 Composite Figures

Find the shaded area. Round to the nearest tenth, if necessary.

10.

11.

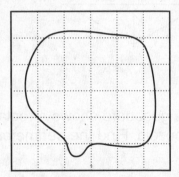

12. A map of an irregularly shaped pond is shown on the grid. The grid has squares with lengths of 1 yd. A clarifying chemical is added to the pond, based on the area of the pond. The chemical costs $13.88 per square yard. Find the total cost of applying the clarifying chemical to the pond.

Geometry

9-4 Perimeter and Area in the Coordinate Plane

Draw and classify the polygon with the given vertices. Find the perimeter and area of the polygon.

13. $A(\ 2, 1)$, $B(5, 1)$, $C(-2, -4)$

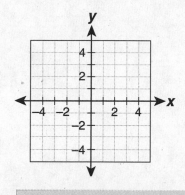

14. $D(-2, 3)$, $E(6, 3)$, $F(6, -3)$, $G(-2, -3)$

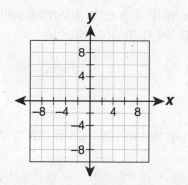

Find the area of each polygon with the given vertices.

15. $H(-3, 3)$, $I(3, 3)$, $J(5, -2)$, $K(-4, -2)$

16. $L(-3, 2)$, $M(4, 2)$, $N(7, -1)$, $P(0, -1)$

9-5 Effects of Changing Dimensions Proportionally

Describe the effect of each change on the perimeter and area of the given figure.

17. The length of each diagonal of the rhombus is halved.

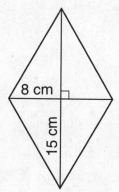

8 cm

15 cm

Geometry

18. The base and height of the parallelogram are both tripled.

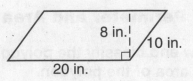

8 in. | 10 in.
20 in.

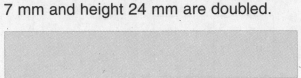

19. The base and height of a right triangle with base 7 mm and height 24 mm are doubled.

20. The radius of a circle with radius 5 cm is doubled.

21. A square has vertices (0, −1), (0, 3), (4, 3) and (4, −1). If the area of the square is doubled, what happens to the side length?

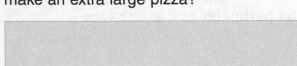

22. A pizza shop specializes in two sizes of pizza, the regular and the extra large. The regular has a 16-in diameter and requires 4 cups of dough. The diameter of the extra large pizza is 20 inches. About how much dough is needed to make an extra large pizza?

Geometry

9-6 Geometric Probability

Use the spinner to find the probability of each event.

23. the pointer landing on red

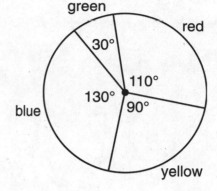

24. the pointer landing on blue or green

25. the pointer not landing on yellow

26. the pointer on yellow, red, or blue

27. A bus makes a stop at an intersection five times each hour. The stops last three minutes each, find the probability that a bus will be waiting if you randomly walk up to the bus stop.

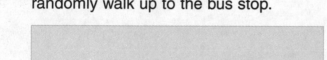

Geometry

Postulates and Theorems

Postulate 1-1-1   (Area Addition Postulate) The area of a region is equal to the sum of the areas of its nonoverlapping parts.

Geometry

Answer these questions to summarize the important concepts from Chapter 9 in your own words.

1. Explain the difference between area and perimeter.

2. Explain what is wrong with the following: To find the area of a parallelogram with sides 8 and 5, multiply 8 by 5 and get a product of 40.

3. Explain the process for finding the area of a composite figure.

4. What are the effects on the area and perimeter of a figure if the dimensions of the figure are multiplied by *n*?

For more review of Chapter 9:

• Complete the Chapter 9 Study Guide and Review on pages 640–643 of your textbook.

• Complete the Ready to Go On quizzes on pages 615 and 639 of your textbook.

Geometry

The table contains important vocabulary terms from Chapter 10. As you work through the chapter, fill in the page number, definition, and a clarifying example.

Term	Page	Definition	Clarifying Example
cone			
cube			
cylinder			
edge of a three-dimensional figure			
face of a polyhedron			
isometric drawing			
orthographic drawing			

Geometry

Term	Page	Definition	Clarifying Example
perspective drawing			
polyhedron			
prism			
pyramid			
sphere			
surface area			
vanishing point			
volume			

Geometry

Solid Geometry

Lesson Objectives (p. 654):

_____

_____

Vocabulary

1. Face (p. 654): _____

_____

2. Edge (p. 654): _____

_____

3. Vertex (p. 654): _____

_____

4. Prism (p. 654): _____

_____

5. Cylinder (p. 654): _____

_____

6. Pyramid (p. 654): _____

_____

7. Cone (p. 654): _____

_____

8. Cube (p. 654): _____

_____

9. Net (p. 655): _____

_____

10. Cross section (p. 656): _____

_____

Geometry

Key Concepts

11. Three-Dimensional Figures (p. 654):

TERM	EXAMPLE
PRISM:	
CYLINDER:	
PYRAMID:	
CONE:	

12. Get Organized Complete the graphic organizer. (p. 656).

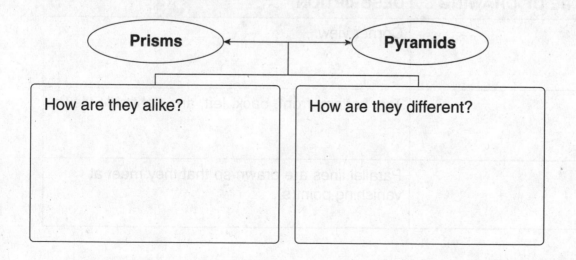

Prisms ← → Pyramids

How are they alike?

How are they different?

Geometry

Representations of Three-Dimensional Figures

LESSON 10-2

Lesson Objectives (p. 661):

_____

_____

Vocabulary

1. Orthographic drawing (p. 661): _____

_____

2. Isometric drawing (p. 662): _____

_____

3. Perspective drawing (p. 662): _____

_____

4. Vanishing point (p. 662): _____

_____

5. Horizon (p. 662): _____

_____

Key Concepts

6. Get Organized Complete the graphic organizer. (p. 664).

TYPE OF DRAWING	DESCRIPTION
	Corner view.
	Top, bottom, front, back, left, and right side views
	Parallel lines are drawn so that they meet at vanishing point(s).

Geometry

Formulas in Three Dimensions

Lesson Objectives (p. 670):

Vocabulary

1. Polyhedron (p. 670): _____

2. Space (p. 671): _____

Key Concepts

3. Euler's Formula (p. 670):

4. Diagonal of a Right Rectangular Prism (p. 671):

5. Distance and Midpoint Formulas in Three Dimensions (p. 672):

Geometry

6. Get Organized Complete the graphic organizer. (p 673).

	RECTANGULAR PRISM	RECTANGULAR PYRAMID
Vertices V		
Edges E		
Faces F		
V − E + F		

Geometry

Surface Area of Prisms and Cylinders

Lesson Objectives (p. 680):

_____

_____

Vocabulary

1. Lateral face (p. 680): _____

_____

2. Lateral edge (p. 680): _____

_____

3. Right prism (p. 680): _____

_____

4. Oblique prism (p. 680): _____

_____

5. Altitude (p. 680): _____

_____

6. Surface area (p. 680): _____

_____

7. Lateral surface (p. 681): _____

_____

8. Axis of a cylinder (p. 681): _____

_____

9. Right cylinder (p. 681): _____

_____

10. Oblique cylinder (p. 681): _____

_____

Key Concepts

11. Lateral Area and Surface Area of Right Prisms (p. 680):

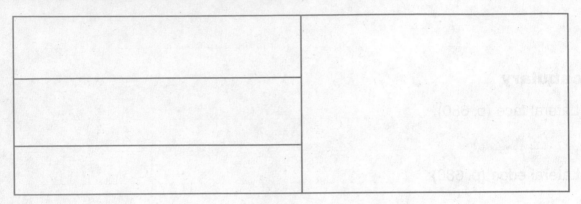

12. Lateral Area and Surface Area of Right Cylinders (p. 681):

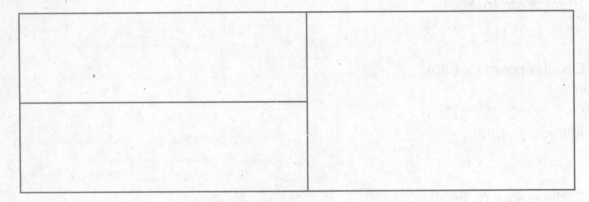

13. Get Organized Write the formulas in each box. (p. 683).

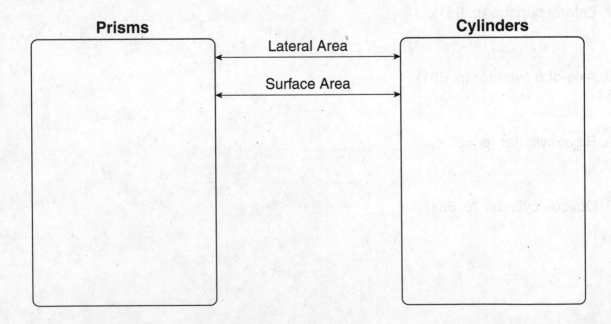

Geometry

Surface Area of Pyramids and Cones

Lesson Objectives (p. 689):

_____

_____

Vocabulary

1. Vertex of a pyramid (p. 689): _____

_____

2. Regular pyramid (p. 689): _____

_____

3. Slant height of a regular pyramid (p. 689): _____

_____

4. Altitude of a pyramid (p. 689): _____

_____

5. Vertex of a cone (p. 690): _____

_____

6. Axis of a cone (p. 690): _____

_____

7. Right cone (p. 690): _____

_____

8. Oblique cone (p. 690): _____

_____

9. Slant height of a right cone (p. 690): _____

_____

10. Altitude of a cone (p. 690): _____

_____

Geometry

Key Concepts

11. Lateral and Surface Area of a Regular Pyramid (p. 689):

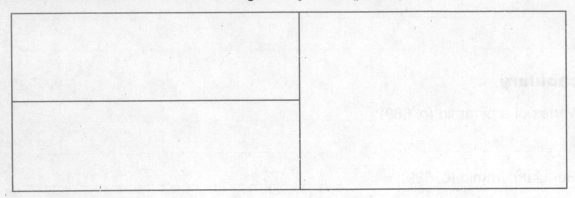

12. Lateral and Surface Area of a Right Cone (p. 690):

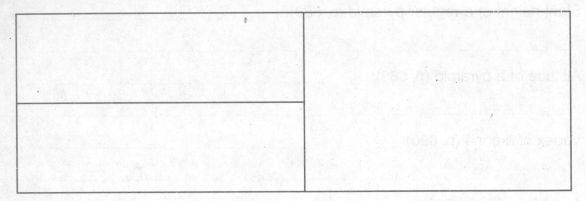

13. Get Organized In each box, write the name of the part of the cone. (p. 692).

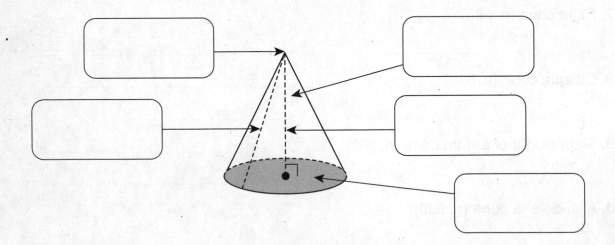

Geometry

Volume of Prisms and Cylinders

Lesson Objectives (p. 697):

_____

_____

Vocabulary

1. Volume (p. 697): _____

_____

Key Concepts

2. Volume of a Prism (p. 697):

3. Volume of a Cylinder (p. 699):

219

Geometry

4. Get Organized In each box, write the formula for the volume. (p. 700).

SHAPE	VOLUME
Prism	
Cube	
Cylinder	

Geometry

Volume of Pyramids and Cones

Lesson Objectives (p. 705):

_____

_____

Key Concepts

1. Volume of a Pyramid (p. 705):

2. Volume of Cones (p. 707):

Geometry

3. Get Organized Complete the graphic organizer. (p. 708).

Volumes of Three-Dimensional Figures		
Formula	$V = Bh$	$V = \frac{1}{3}Bh$
Shapes		
Example		

Geometry

Spheres

Lesson Objectives (p. 714):

_____

_____

Vocabulary

1. Sphere (p. 714): _____

_____

2. Center of a sphere (p. 714): _____

_____

3. Radius of a sphere (p. 714): _____

_____

4. Hemisphere (p. 714): _____

_____

5. Great circle (p. 714): _____

_____

Key Concepts

6. Volume of a Sphere (p. 714):

Geometry

7. Surface Area of a Sphere (p. 716):

8. Get Organized Complete the graphic organizer. (p. 717).

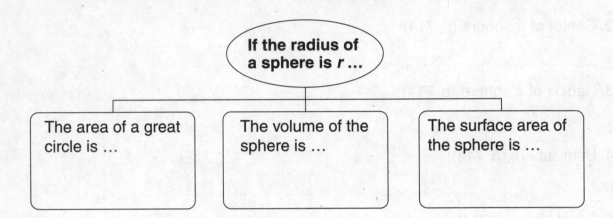

Geometry

10-1 Solid Geometry

Classify each figure. Name the vertices, edges and bases.

1.
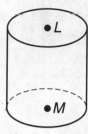

2.
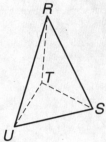

3.
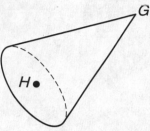

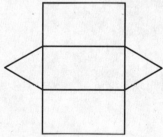

Describe the three-dimensional figure that can be made from the given net.

4.

5.

6.
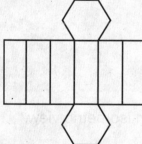

Geometry

Describe the cross section.

7.

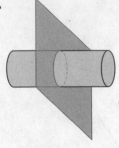

8.

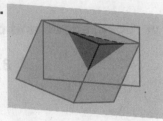

9.

10-2 Representations of Three-Dimensional Figures

Use the figure made of unit cube for Problems 10 and 11. Assume there are no hidden cubes.

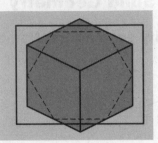

10. Draw all six orthographic views.

11. Draw an isometric view.

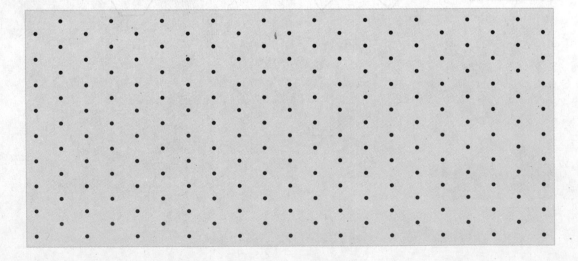

Geometry

12. Draw the block letter F in one-point perspective.

13. Draw the block letter F in two-point perspective.

10-3 Formulas in Three Dimensions

Find the number of vertices, edges, and faces of each polyhedron. Use your results to verify the Euler's formula.

14. rectangular prism

15. pentagonal pyramid

16. rectangular pyramid

17. A fish tank is in the shape of a rectangular prism. The base of the fish tank is 2 ft by 3 ft and has a 4.5 ft diagonal. What is the height of the fish tank?

Geometry

Find the distance between the given points. Find the midpoint of the segments with the given end points. Round to the nearest tenth, if necessary.

18. (0, 0, 0) and (6, 8, 12)

19. (4, 1, −1) and (3, −3, 5)

20. (5, 6, −2) and (4, −2, 6)

10-4 Surface Area of Prisms and Cylinders

Find the surface area of each figure. Round to the nearest tenth, if necessary.

21.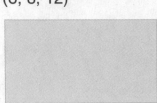
5 in.
24 in.
30 in.

22.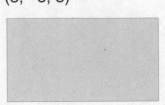
6 ft
4 ft

23.
2 in.
5 in.
4 in.
6 in.

24. The dimensions of a 12 in. by 9 in. by 24 in. right rectangular prism are multiplied by $\frac{2}{3}$. Describe the affect on the surface area.

10-5 Surface Area of Pyramids and Cones

Find the surface area of each figure. Round to the nearest tenth, if necessary.

25. a regular square pyramid with base edge length of 6 ft and slant height 14 ft

26. a right cone with diameter 32 cm and height 18 cm

Geometry

27. the composite figure formed by a cone and a cylinder

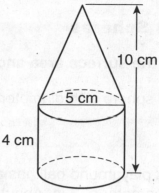

10 cm

5 cm

4 cm

10-6 Volume of Prisms and Cylinders

Find the volume of each figure. Round to the nearest tenth if necessary.

28. a regular hexagonal prism with base area 192 in.^{2} and height 24 in.

29. a cylinder with radius 3 yd and height 11 yd

30. A brick patio measures 8 ft by 10 ft by 3 in. Find the volume of the bricks. If the density of a brick is about 140 pounds per cubic foot, what is the weight of the patio in pounds?

31. The dimensions of a cylinder with diameter 2 ft and height 1 ft are reduced by half. Describe the affect on the volume.

10-7 Volume of Pyramids and Cones

Find the volume of each figure. Round to the nearest tenth, if necessary.

32.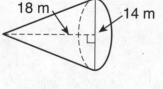
18 m   14 m

33.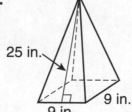
25 in.
9 in.
9 in.

34.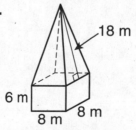
18 m
6 m
8 m   8 m

Geometry

10-8 Spheres

Find the surface area and the volume of each figure.

35. a sphere with diameter 6 in.

36. a hemisphere with radius 5 cm

37. A playground ball has a diameter of about 9 in. A bouncy ball has the diameter of 3 in. About how many more times as great is the volume of the playground ball as the volume of a bouncy ball?

Answer these questions to summarize the important concepts from Chapter 10 in your own words.

1. Name the six different views of an object in an orthographic drawing.

2. Describe how you can find the distance between two points (x_1, y_1, z_1) and (x_2, y_2, z_2).

3. Describe the difference between surface area and lateral area.

4. Describe how the volume of a cone is related to the volume of a cylinder.

For more review of Chapter 10:

- Complete the Chapter 10 Study Guide and Review on pages 730–733 of your textbook.

- Complete the Ready to Go On quizzes on pages 679 and 725 of your textbook.

Geometry

Vocabulary

The table contains important vocabulary terms from Chapter 11. As you work through the chapter, fill in the page number, definition, and a clarifying example.

Term	Page	Definition	Clarifying Example
adjacent arcs			
arc			
arc length			
central angle of circle			
chord			
common tangent			

Geometry

Term	Page	Definition	Clarifying Example
intercepted arc			
major arc			
minor arc			
point of tangency			
secant of a circle			
sector of a circle			
segment of a circle			
semicircle			
tangent of a circle			

233

Geometry

Lines That Intersect Circles

Lesson Objectives (p. 746):

_____

_____

Vocabulary

1. Interior of a circle (p. 746): _____

_____

2. Exterior of a circle (p. 746): _____

_____

3. Chord (p. 746): _____

_____

4. Secant (p. 746): _____

_____

5. Tangent of a circle (p. 746): _____

_____

6. Point of tangency (p. 746): _____

_____

7. Congruent circles (p. 747): _____

_____

8. Concentric circles (p. 747): _____

_____

9. Tangent circles (p. 747): _____

_____

10. Common tangent (p. 748): _____

_____

Geometry

Key Concepts

11. Lines and Segments That Intersect Circles (p. 746):

TERM	DIAGRAM
CHORD	
SECANT	
TANGENT	
POINT OF TANGENCY	

12. Pairs of Circles (p. 747):

TERM	DIAGRAM
CONGRUENT CIRCLES	
CONCENTRIC CIRCLES	
TANGENT CIRCLES	

Geometry

13. Theorems (p. 748):

THEOREM	HYPOTHESIS	CONCLUSION
11-1-1		
11-1-2		

14. Theorem 11-1-3 (p. 749):

THEOREM	HYPOTHESIS	CONCLUSION
11-1-3		

Geometry

15. Get Organized In each box, write a definition and draw a sketch. (p. 750).

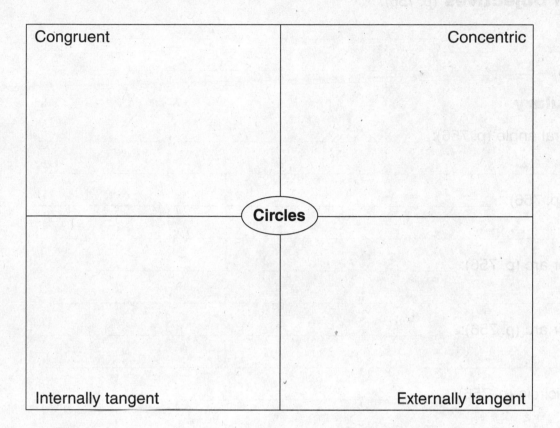

Congruent	Concentric
Internally tangent	Externally tangent

Circles

Arcs and Chords

Lesson Objectives (p. 756):

_____

_____

Vocabulary

1. Central angle (p. 756): _____

_____

2. Arc (p. 756): _____

_____

3. Minor arc (p. 756): _____

_____

4. Major arc (p. 756): _____

_____

5. Semicircle (p. 756): _____

_____

6. Adjacent arcs (p. 757): _____

_____

7. Congruent arcs (p. 757): _____

_____

Geometry

Key Concepts

8. Arcs and Their Measure (p. 756):

ARC	MEASURE	DIAGRAM
Minor arc		
Major arc		
Semicircle		

9. Postulate 11-2-1—Arc Addition Postulate (p. 757):

Postulate 11-2-1

Geometry

10. Theorem 11-2-2 (p. 757):

THEOREM	HYPOTHESIS	CONCLUSION
In a circle or congruent circles:		

11. Theorems (p. 759):

THEOREM	HYPOTHESIS	CONCLUSION
11-2-3		
11-2-4		

Geometry

12. Get Organized In each box write a definition and draw a sketch. (p. 759).

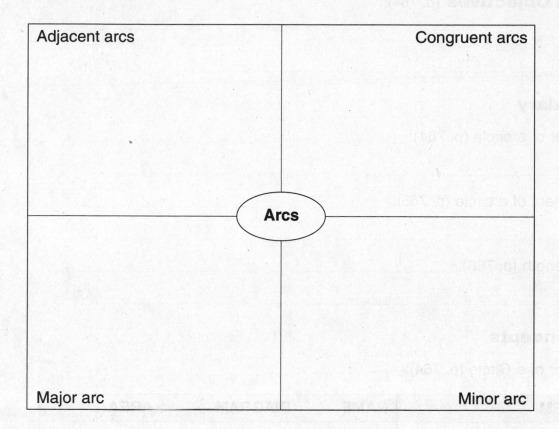

Adjacent arcs	Congruent arcs

Arcs

Major arc	Minor arc

Geometry

Sector Area and Arc Length

Lesson Objectives (p. 764):

_____

_____

Vocabulary

1. Sector of a circle (p. 764): _____

_____

2. Segment of a circle (p. 765): _____

_____

3. Arc length (p. 766): _____

_____

Key Concepts

4. Sector of a Circle (p. 764):

TERM	NAME	DIAGRAM	AREA

5. Area of a Segment (p. 765):

6. Arc Length (p. 766):

TERM	DIAGRAM	LENGTH

7. Get Organized Complete the graphic organizer. (p. 766).

	FORMULA	DIAGRAM
Area of a Sector		
Area of a Segment		
Arc Length		

Geometry

Inscribed Angles

Lesson Objectives (p. 772):

_____

_____

Vocabulary

1. Inscribed angle (p. 772): _____

_____

2. Intercepted arc (p. 772): _____

_____

3. Subtend (p. 772): _____

Key Concepts

4. Theorem 11-4-1—Inscribed Angle Theorem (p. 772):

Theorem 11-4-1

5. Corollary 11-4-2 (p. 773):

COROLLARY	HYPOTHESIS	CONCLUSION

Geometry

6. Theorem 11-4-3 (p. 774):

Theorem 11-4-3

7. Theorem 11-4-4 (p. 775):

THEOREM	HYPOTHESIS	CONCLUSION

8. Get Organized Complete the graphic organizer. (p. 775).

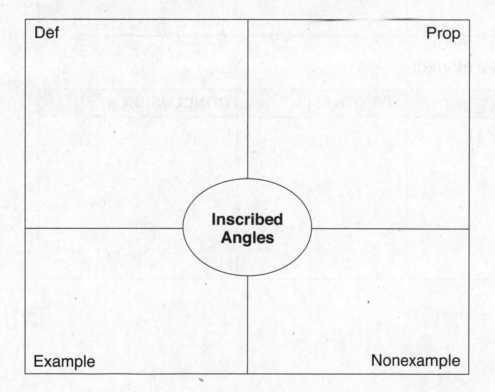

Angle Relationships in Circles

Lesson Objectives (p. 782):

_____

_____

Key Concepts

1. Theorem 11-5-1 (p. 782):

THEOREM	HYPOTHESIS	CONCLUSION

2. Theorem 11-5-2 (p. 783):

THEOREM	HYPOTHESIS	CONCLUSION

Geometry

3. Theorem 11-5-3 (p. 784):

Theorem 11-5-3

4. Angle Relationships in Circles (p. 785):

VERTEX OF THE ANGLE	MEASURE OF ANGLE	DIAGRAMS

Geometry

5. Get Organized Fill in each box by writing a theorem and drawing a diagram according to where the angle's vertex is in relationship to the circle. (p. 786).

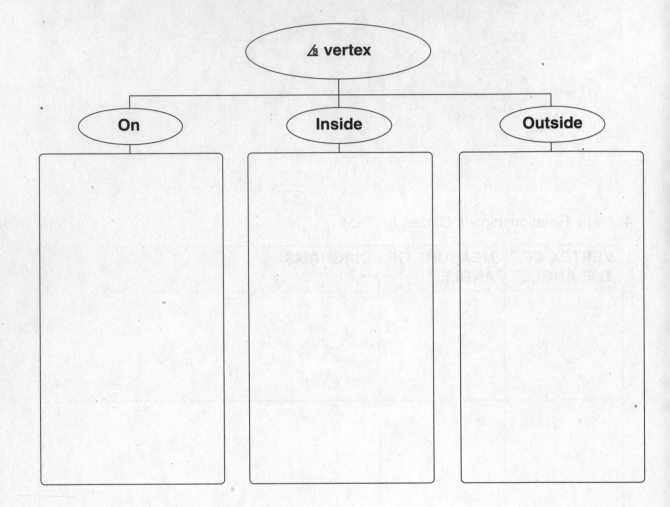

Geometry

Segment Relationships in Circles

Lesson Objectives (p. 792):

_____

_____

Vocabulary

1. Secant segment (p. 793): _____

_____

2. External secant segment (p. 793): _____

_____

3. Tangent segment (p. 794): _____

_____

Key Concepts

4. Theorem 11-6-1—Chord-Chord Product Theorem (p. 792):

THEOREM	HYPOTHESIS	CONCLUSION

5. Theorem 11-6-2—Secant-Secant Product Theorem (p. 793):

THEOREM	HYPOTHESIS	CONCLUSION

6. Theorem 11-6-3—Secant-Tangent Product Theorem (p. 794):

THEOREM	HYPOTHESIS	CONCLUSION

Geometry

7. Get Organized Complete the graphic organizer. (p. 795).

	THEOREM	DIAGRAM	EXAMPLE
Chord-Chord			
Secant-Secant			
Secant-Tangent			

Geometry

LESSON 11-7

Circles in the Coordinate Plane

Lesson Objectives (p. 799):

_____

_____

Key Concepts

1. Theorem 11-7-1—Equation of a Circle (p. 799):

2. **Get Organized** Select values for a center and radius. Then use the center and radius you wrote to fill in the circles. Write the corresponding equation and draw the corresponding graph (p. 801).

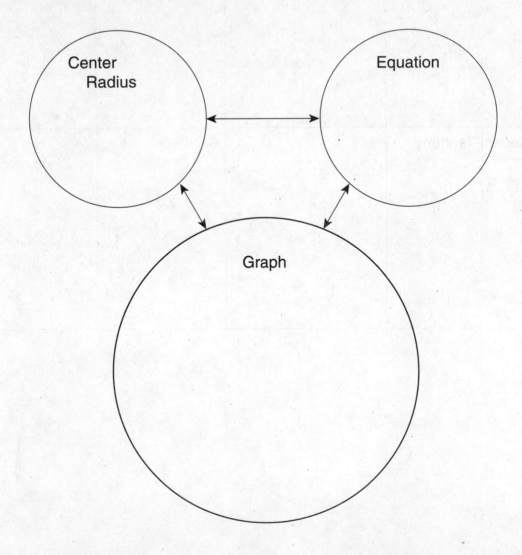

Center
Radius

Equation

Graph

Geometry

11-1 Lines that Intersect Circles

Identify each line or segment that intersects each circle.

1.

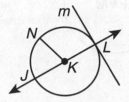

2.

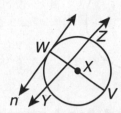

3. The summit of Mt. McKinley in Alaska is about 20,321 feet above sea level. What is the distance from the summit to the horizon, to the nearest mile?
(Hint: 5280 ft = 1 mile, radius of the Earth = 4000 miles)

11-2 Arcs and Chords

Find each measurement.

4. $\overset{\frown}{FB}$

5. $\overset{\frown}{BEC}$

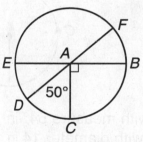

6. $\overset{\frown}{FG}$

7. $\overset{\frown}{FCA}$

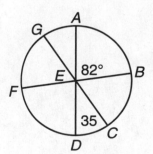

Find each length to the nearest tenth.

8. *AC*

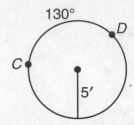

9. *JK*

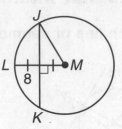

11-3 Sector Area and Arc Length

Find the shaded area. Round to the nearest tenth, if necessary.

10. As part of a parks beautification committee Kelly is designing a circular flower garden. She plans to divide the flower garden into sectors and plant different colored flowers in each sector. What is the area of each sector to the nearest square foot?

Find each arc length. Give your answer in terms of π and rounded to the nearest hundredth.

11. $\overset{\frown}{CD}$

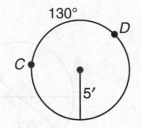

12. $\overset{\frown}{FG}$

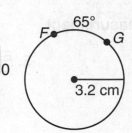

13. an arc with measure 54° in a circle with diameter 14 in.

14. a semicircle in a circle with diameter 112 m

Geometry

11-4 Inscribed Angles

Find each measure.

15. m∠ADB

16. m⌢CB

For Problems 15 and 16.

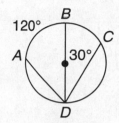

For Problems 17 and 18.

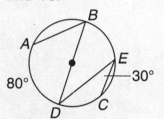

17. m∠ABD

18. m⌢DC

11-5 Angle Relationships in Circles

Find each measure.

19. m∠LMN

20. m∠AFD

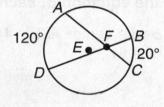

21. Find the measure of angle *x*.

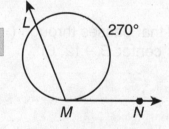

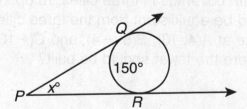

Geometry

11-6 Segment Relationships in Circles

Find the value of the variable and the length of each chord or secant segment.

22.

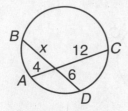

23.

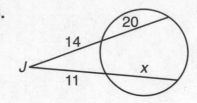

24. A section of an arched bridge is based on an arc of a circle as shown. $\overline{BD}$ is the perpendicular bisector of $\overline{AC}$. $AC = 60$ ft, and $BD = 20$ ft. What is the diameter of the circle?

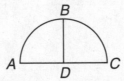

11-7 Circles in the Coordinate Plane

Write the equation of each circle.

25. $\odot B$ with center $A(3, -4)$ and radius 5

26. $\odot B$ that passes through $(-4, 12)$ has center $B(-12, 6)$

27. A local technology company is planning the location of a new cell phone tower to help with coverage in three cities. To optimize cell phone coverage, the tower should be equidistant from the three cities which are located on a coordinate plane at $A(4, 10)$, $B(6, -4)$, and $C(-10, -4)$. What are the coordinates where the tower should be built?

Geometry

Theorem 11-1-1   If a line is tangent to a circle, then it is perpendicular to the radius drawn to the point of tangency. (line tangent to ⊙ → line ⊥ to radius)

Theorem 11-1-2   If a line is perpendicular to a radius of a circle at a point on the circle, then the line is tangent to the circle. (line ⊥ to radius → line tangent to ⊙)

Theorem 11-1-3   If two segments are tangent to a circle, from the same external point, then the segments are congruent.
(2 segs. tangent to ⊙ from same ext. pt. → segs ≅)

Postulate 11-2-1   (Arc Addition Postulate) The measure of an arc formed by two adjacent arcs is the sum of the measure of the two arcs.

Theorem 11-2-2   In a circle or congruent circles: (1) Congruent central angles have congruent chords. (2) Congruent chords have congruent arcs. (3) Congruent arcs have congruent central angles.

Theorem 11-2-3   In a circle, if a radius (or diameter) is perpendicular to a chord, then it bisects the chord and its arc.

Theorem 11-2-4   In a circle, the perpendicular bisector of a chord is a radius (or a diameter).

Theorem 11-4-1   The measure of an inscribed angle is half the measure of its intercepted arc.

Corollary 11-4-2   If inscribed angles of a circle intercept the same arc or are subtended by the same chord or arc, then the angles are congruent.

Theorem 11-4-3   An inscribed angle subtends a semicircle if and only if the angle is a right angle.

Theorem 11-4-4   If a quadrilateral is inscribed in a circle, then its opposite angles are supplementary.

Theorem 11-5-1   If a tangent and a secant (or chord) intersect on a circle at the point of tangency, then the measure of the angle formed is half the measure of its intercepted arc.

Theorem 11-5-2   If two secants or chords intersect in the interior of a circle, then the measure of each angle formed is half the sum of the measures of its intercepted arcs.

Geometry

Theorem 11-5-3   If a tangent and a secant, two tangents, or two secants intersect in the exterior of a circle, then the measure of the angle formed is half the difference of the measures of its intercepted arcs.

Theorem 11-6-1   (Chord-Chord Product Theorem) If two chords intersect in the interior of a circle, then the products of the lengths of the segments of the chords are equal.

Theorem 11-6-2   (Secant-Secant Product Theorem) If two secants intersect in the exterior of a circle, then the product of the lengths of one secant segment and its external segment equals the product of the lengths of the other secant segment and its external segment. (whole · outside = whole · outside)

Theorem 11-6-3   (Secant-Tangent Product Theorem) If a secant and a tangent intersect in the exterior of a circle, then the product of the lengths of the secant segment and its external segment equals the length of the tangent segment squared. (whole · outside = tangent^2)

Theorem 11-7-1   (Equation of a Circle) The equation of a circle with center (h, k) and radius r is $(x - h)^2 + (y - k)^2 = r^2$.

Geometry

Answer these questions to summarize the important concepts from Chapter 11 in your own words.

1. Explain the relationship between central angles and chords.

2. Explain how to find the area of a sector.

3. Explain the different angle relationships in circles.

4. What are the relationships between segments in a circle?

For more review of Chapter 11:

- Complete the Chapter 11 Study Guide and Review on pages 810–813 of your textbook.

- Complete the Ready to Go On quizzes on pages 771 and 807 of your textbook.

Geometry

Vocabulary

The table contains important vocabulary terms from Chapter 12. As you work through the chapter, fill in the page number, definition, and a clarifying example.

Term	Page	Definition	Clarifying Example
center of dilation			
composition of transformations			
enlargement			
glide reflection			
isometry			
line of symmetry			

Geometry

Term	Page	Definition	Clarifying Example
line symmetry			
reduction			
rotational symmetry			
symmetry			
tessellation			
translation symmetry			

Geometry

LESSON
12-1

Reflections

Lesson Objectives (p. 824):

_____

Vocabulary

1. Isometry (p. 824): _____

_____

Key Concepts

2. Reflections (p. 825):

3. Reflections in the Coordinate Plane (p. 826):

ACROSS THE x-axis	ACROSS THE y-axis	ACROSS THE $y = x$

4. Get Organized Complete the graphic organizer. (p. 826).

LINE OF REFLECTION	IMAGE OF (a, b)	EXAMPLE
x-axis		
y-axis		
$y = x$		

Geometry

Translations

Lesson Objectives (p. 831):

_____

_____

Key Concepts

1. Translations (p. 832):

2. Translations in the Coordinate Plane (p. 832):

HORIZONTAL TRANSLATION ALONG VECTOR (*a*, 0)	VERTICAL TRANSLATION ALONG VECTOR (0, *b*)	GENERAL TRANSLATION ALONG VECTOR (*a*, *b*)

Geometry

3. Get Organized Complete the graphic organizer. (p. 833).

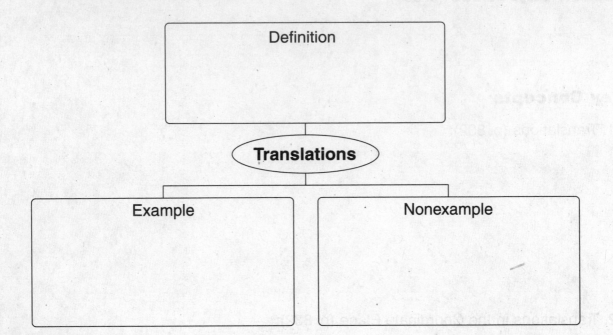

Rotations

Lesson Objectives (p. 839):

_____

_____

Key Concepts

1. Rotation (p. 840):

2. Rotations in the Coordinate Plane (p. 840):

BY 90° ABOUT THE ORIGIN	BY 180° ABOUT THE ORIGIN

Geometry

3. Get Organized Complete the graphic organizer. (p. 841).

	REFLECTION	TRANSLATION	ROTATION
Definition			
Example			

Geometry

Compositions of Transformations

LESSON
12-4

Lesson Objectives (p. 848):

_____

_____

Vocabulary

1. Composition of transformations (p. 848): _____

_____

2. Glide reflection (p. 848): _____

_____

Key Concepts

3. Theorem 12-4-1 (p. 848):

Theorem 12-4-1

4. Theorem 12-4-2 (p. 849):

5. Theorem 12-4-3 (p. 850):

6. Get Organized In each box, describe an equivalent transformation and sketch an example. (p. 850).

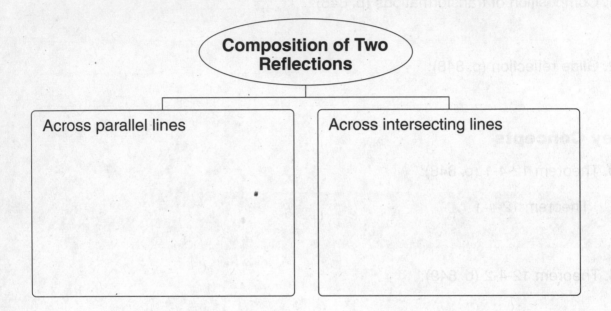

Composition of Two Reflections

Across parallel lines

Across intersecting lines

Geometry

Symmetry

Lesson Objectives (p. 856):

_____

_____

Vocabulary

1. Symmetry (p. 856): _____

_____

2. Line symmetry (p. 856): _____

_____

3. Line of symmetry (p. 856): _____

_____

4. Rotational symmetry (p. 857): _____

_____

_____

Key Concepts

5. Line Symmetry (p. 856):

6. Rotational Symmetry (p. 857):

7. Get Organized In each region, draw a figure with the given type of symmetry. (p. 858).

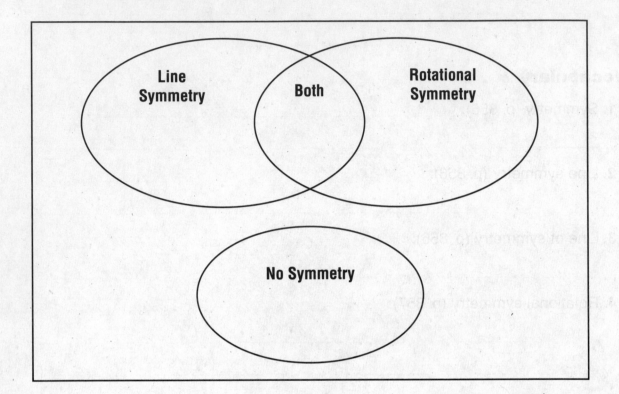

LESSON 12-6 — Tessellations

Lesson Objectives (p. 863):

_____

_____

Vocabulary

1. Translation symmetry (p. 863): _____

_____

2. Frieze pattern (p. 863): _____

_____

3. Glide reflection symmetry (p. 863): _____

_____

4. Tessellation (p. 863): _____

_____

5. Regular tessellation (p. 864): _____

_____

6. Semiregular tessellation (p. 864): _____

_____

Key Concepts

7. Get Organized Complete the graphic organizer. (p. 866).

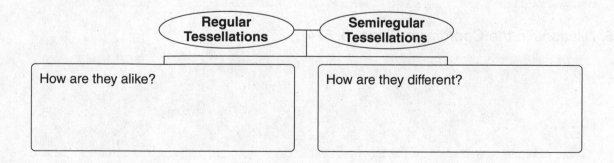

Dilations

Lesson Objectives (p. 872):

_____

_____

Vocabulary

1. Center of dilation (p. 873): _____

_____

2. Enlargement (p. 873): _____

_____

3. Reduction (p. 873): _____

_____

Key Concepts

4. Dilations (p. 873):

5. Dilations in the Coordinate Plane (p. 874):

Geometry

6. Get Organized Select values for a center and radius. Then use the center and radius you wrote to fill in the circles. Write the corresponding equation and draw the corresponding graph (p. 801).

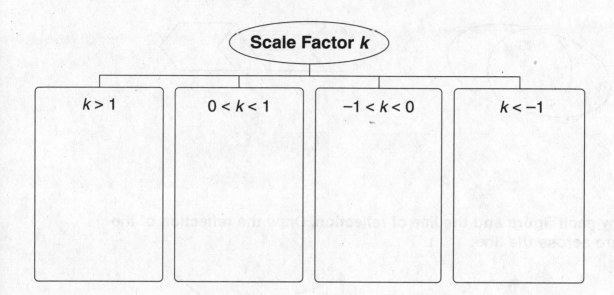

Scale Factor k

| $k > 1$ | $0 < k < 1$ | $-1 < k < 0$ | $k < -1$ |

Geometry

12-1 Reflections

Tell whether each transformation appears to be a reflection.

1.

2.

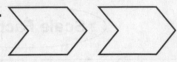

Copy each figure and the line of reflection. Draw the reflection of the figure across the line.

3.

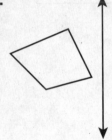

4.

Geometry

Tell whether each formation appears to be a translation.

5.

6.

7. An interior decorator represents a mural on a wall with a rectangle with vertices (4, 1), (7, 1), (7, 5) and (4, 5). She decides to move the mural on the wall to a new location by translating along the vector $\langle -3, 2 \rangle$. Draw the mural in its final position.

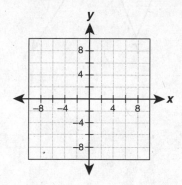

12-3 Rotations

Tell whether the transformation appears to be a rotation.

8.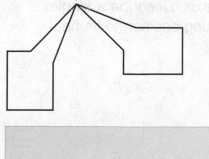

9.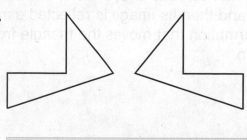

Geometry

Rotate each figure with the given vertices about the origin using the given angles of rotation.

10. $A(1, 2)$, $B(3, 2)$, $C(4, 0)$, $D(0, 0)$; $180°$

11. $A(2, 5)$, $B(4, 2)$, $C(-2, 0)$; $90°$

12-4 Compositions of Transformations

12. Draw the result of the following composition of transformations. Translate *RSTU* along $\vec{V}$ and then reflect it across line *k*.

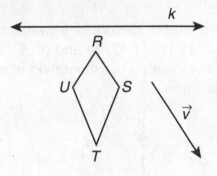

13. $\triangle DEF$ with vertices $D(3, 5)$, $E(6, 1)$ and $F(1, 3)$ is reflected across the *y*-axis and then its image is reflected across the *x*-axis. Describe a single transformation that moves the triangle from its starting position to its final position.

Geometry

12-5 Symmetry

Explain whether each figure has a line of symmetry. If so, copy the figure and draw all lines of symmetry.

14.
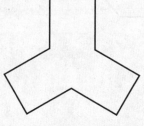

15.
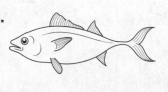

16.

Explain whether each figure has rotation symmetry. If so, give the angle of rotation symmetry and the order of the symmetry.

17.
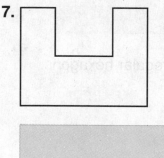

18.

19.

Geometry

12-6 Tessellations

Copy the given figure and use it to create a tessellation.

20.

21.

22.

Classify each tessellation as regular, semiregular, or neither.

23.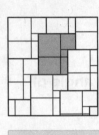

24.

25.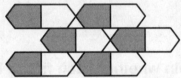

26. Determine whether it is possible to tessellate a plane with regular hexagons. If so, draw the tessellation. If not, explain why.

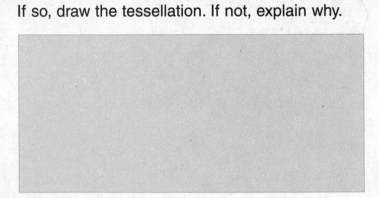

Geometry

12-7 Dilations

Tell whether each transformation appears to be a dilation.

27.

28.

29.

Draw the image of the figure with the given vertices under a dilation with the given scale factor centered at the origin.

30. *R*(2, 3), *S*(3, 5) and *T*(5, 5); scale factor: 2

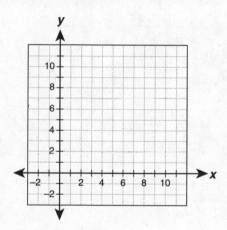

31. *A*(–8, 6), *B*(–8, 4), *C*(1, 6), *D*(1, 4); Scale factor: $-\frac{1}{2}$

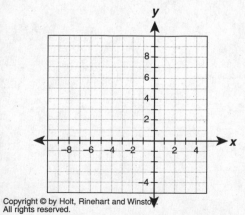

Geometry

Postulates and Theorems

Theorem 12-4-1	A composition of two isometries is an isometry.
Theorem 12-4-2	The composition of two reflections across two parallel lines is equivalent to a translation.

  • The translation vector is perpendicular to the lines.

  • The length of the translation vector is twice the distance between the lines.

The composition of two reflections across two intersecting lines is equivalent to a rotation.

  • The center of rotation is the intersection of the lines.

  • The angle of rotation is twice the measure of the angle formed by the lines.

Theorem 12-4-3	Any translation or rotation is equivalent to a composition of two reflections.

Geometry

Big Ideas

Answer these questions to summarize the important concepts from Chapter 12 in your own words.

1. Describe an isometry and give three examples.

2. Describe the composition of two reflections across two parallel lines in terms of the vector.

3. Describe the composition of two reflections across two intersecting lines in terms of its center and angle.

4. Describe how a figure is dilated in terms of size and shape.

For more review of Chapter 12:

- Complete the Chapter 12 Study Guide and Review on pages 884–887 of your textbook.

- Complete the Ready to Go On quizzes on pages 855 and 881 of your textbook.

Geometry